Models Matter

DAMIANI

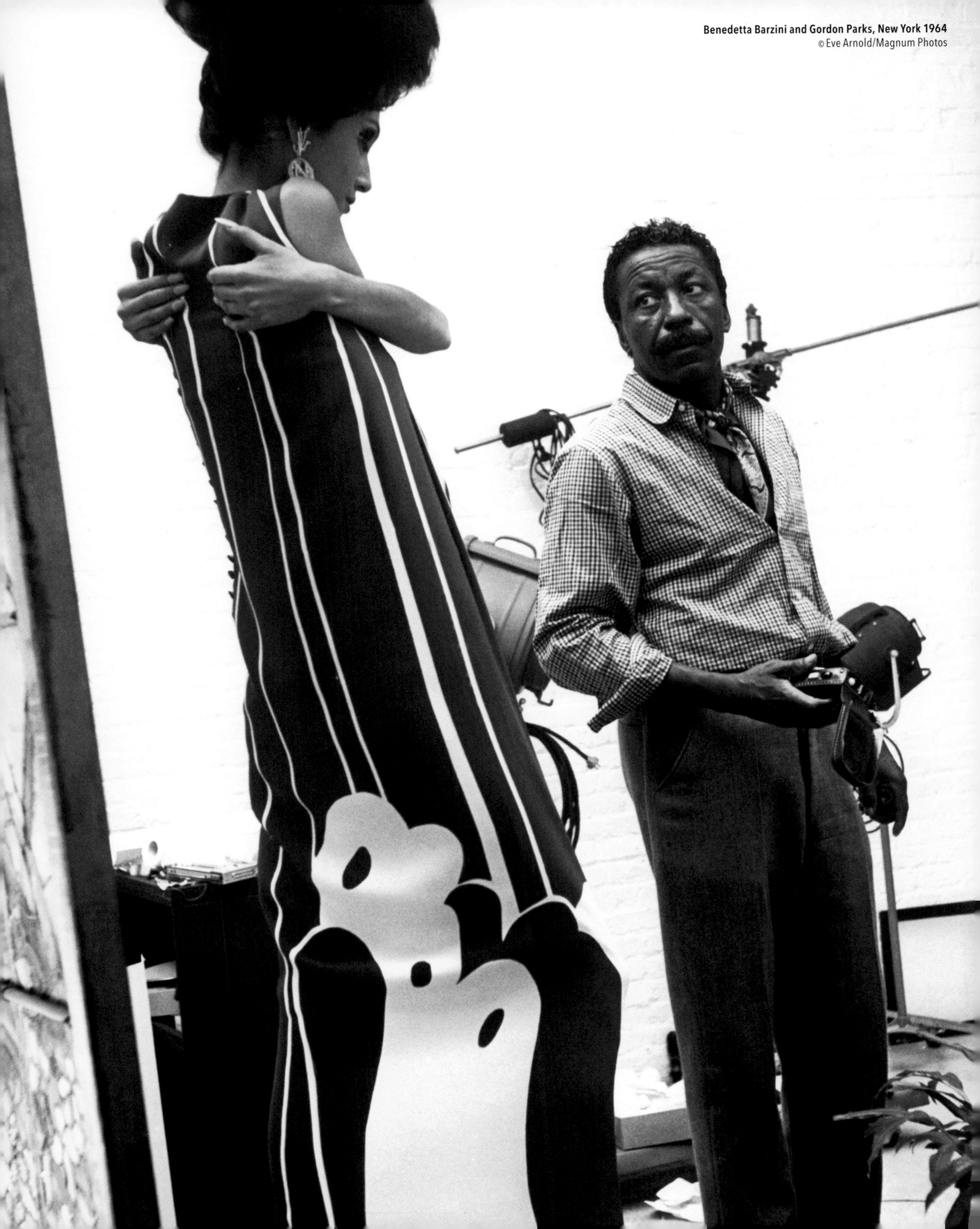

Benedetta Barzini and Gordon Parks, New York 1964
© Eve Arnold/Magnum Photos

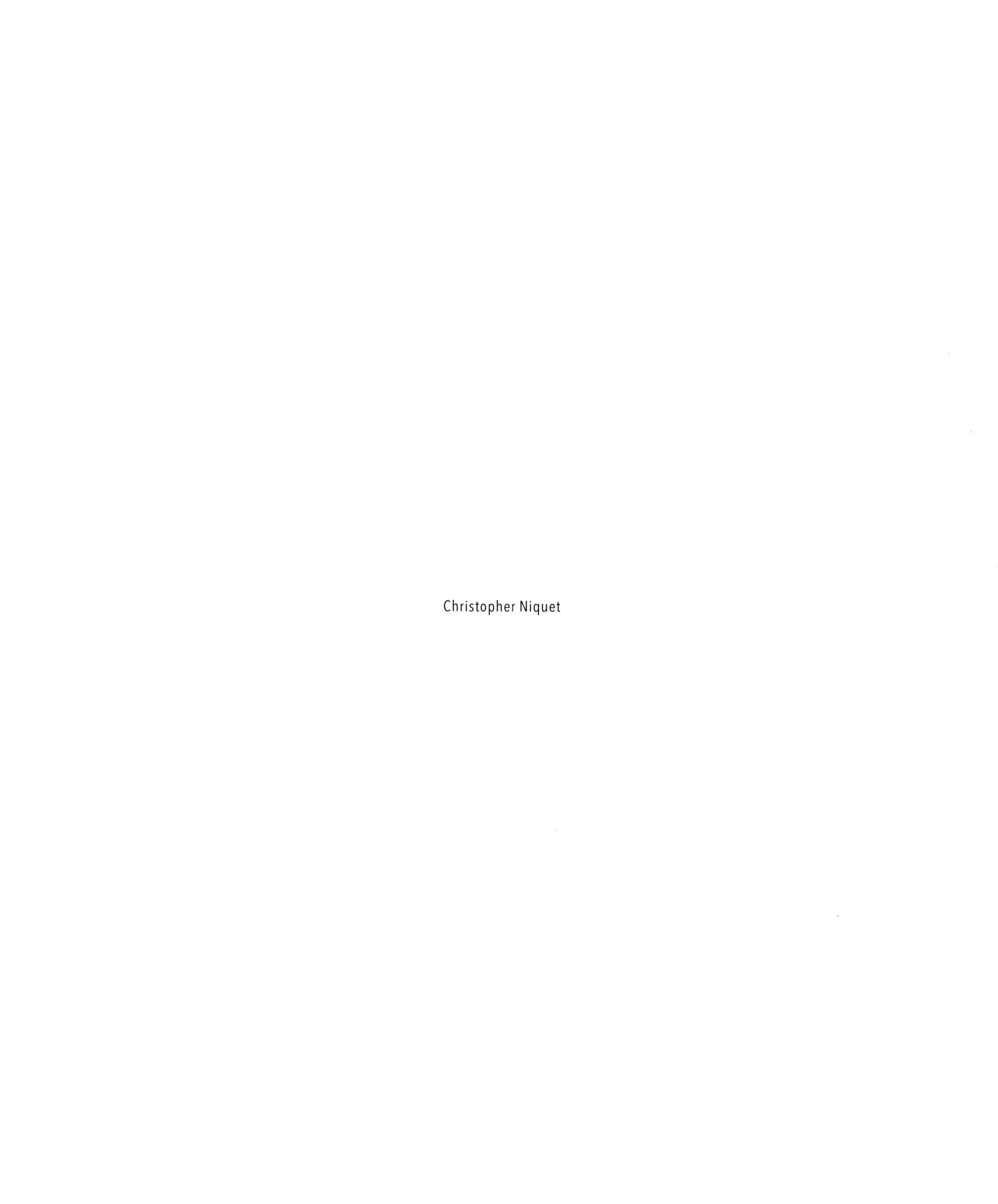

Christopher Niquet

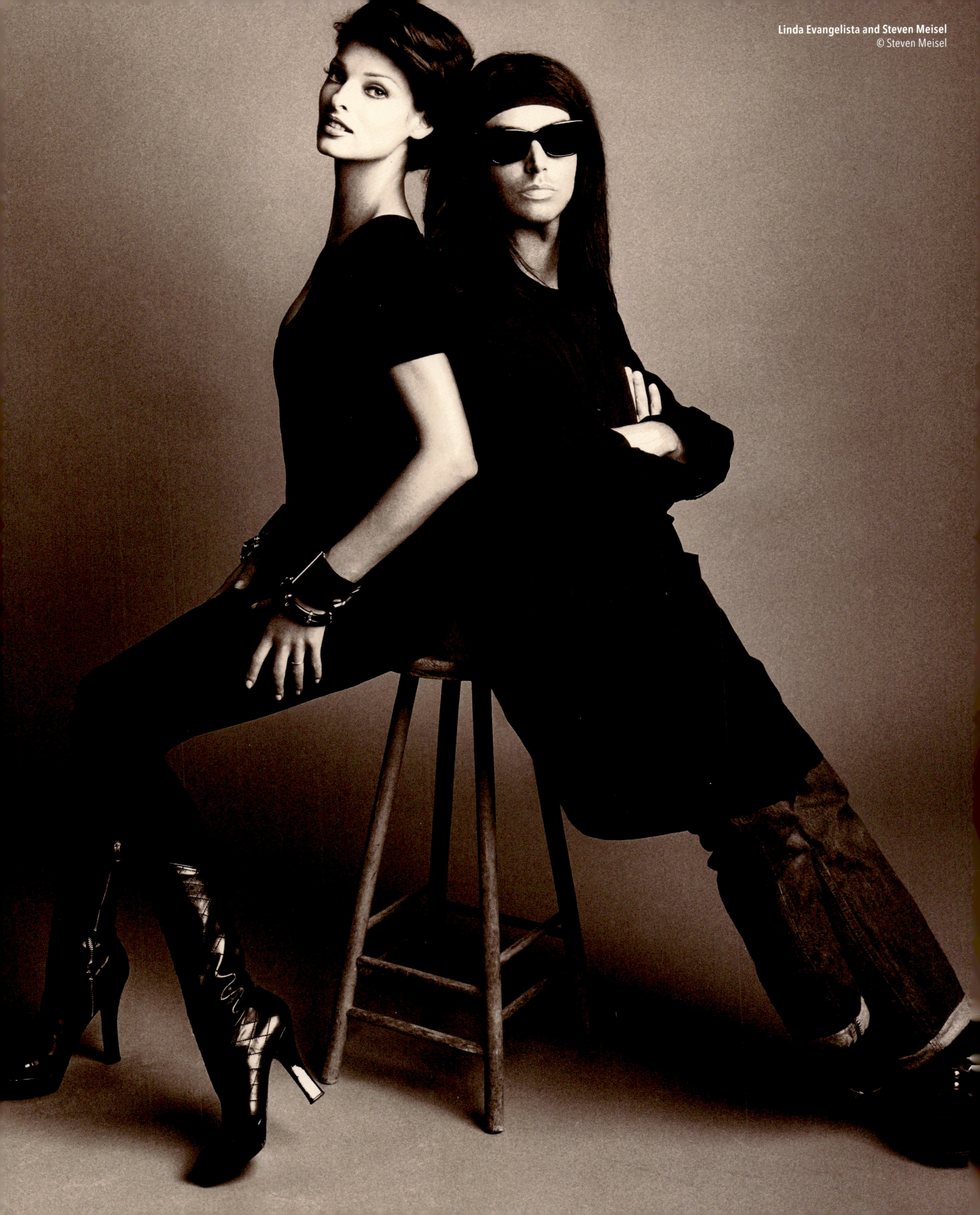
Linda Evangelista and Steven Meisel
© Steven Meisel

The Gatekeepers of My Fantasy World

I first saw Donna Mitchell on a rainy, gloomy New York winter's day. I spotted her two blocks away on East 57th Street, walking toward me in a huge black cape, long crazy hair, full face of makeup, lost in her own film noir. Models used to prep themselves, at home; she was probably on her way to a booking. I was fifteen, and as she passed by me I fell under her spell. It was as if she had stepped out of one of my issues of *Vogue* or *Harper's Bazaar*.

I have loved models since fourth grade. In the Sixties and Seventies they were not household names. They were not credited in the magazines; they had no platform, no social media. Thanks to the magic of New York, I'd see them randomly all the time: Samantha Jones waiting for the elevator at Saks, Marisa Berenson outside my high school, Loulou de la Falaise just passing by. Gradually, I summoned up the courage to take pictures of them in the street, without asking permission. When my cousin offered to take me to Sokolsky's studio, I was petrified, but of course I went. I ended up spending the whole time in the hair and makeup room. I was fascinated by the preparation process, the creation.

I'm often asked what special quality makes a model. I can't answer that question; I just feel it. If I have one talent, this is it: I know instinctively how she will respond to my camera. A great model is a great thespian who puts her trust in me. She takes my cues and adds her own vibrato; this transcends us both. During the golden age of Christy, Naomi, and Linda, my all-white studio on Park Avenue was nicknamed the Clinic. There, we performed a kind of alchemy. It was a place to create, a place to discover. I am forever grateful to those hardworking souls who let me pluck out their eyebrows and cut or dye their hair. Who had the grace and courage to trust me.

Nowadays, models have become overexposed, marketed, disposable. Fashion is still obsessed with the young and the new. Yet, glamour ages well! It was a great pleasure to put Lauren Hutton back to work at forty-six, for Barneys. Incredible, too, to work with the legends of the Sixties and Seventies: Peggy Moffitt, Veruschka, Wallis Franken.

It saddens me that so many voiceless faces from the Fifties to the late Eighties have faded into oblivion. Until I met Christopher Niquet, I thought I was their only admirer, the only archivist of their stories. The fact that someone as young as Christopher cares about Susan Moncur's legacy is cause for amazement, relief, and hope. These women deserve our recognition. They were all so unique, so talented, so passionate about their craft. How could I forget them?

As Linda Evangelista once said, "I serve." This never ceases to humble me.

Steven Meisel

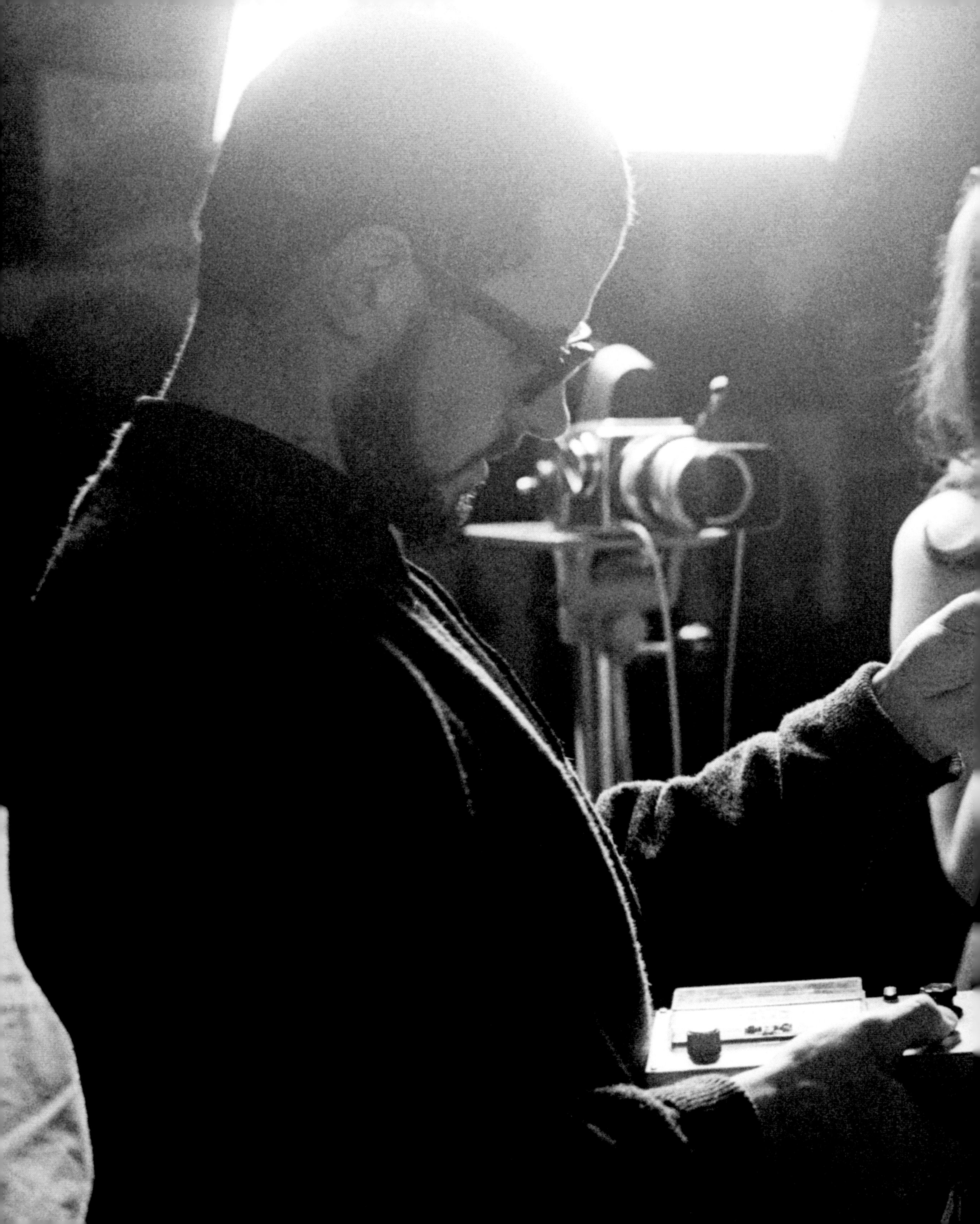

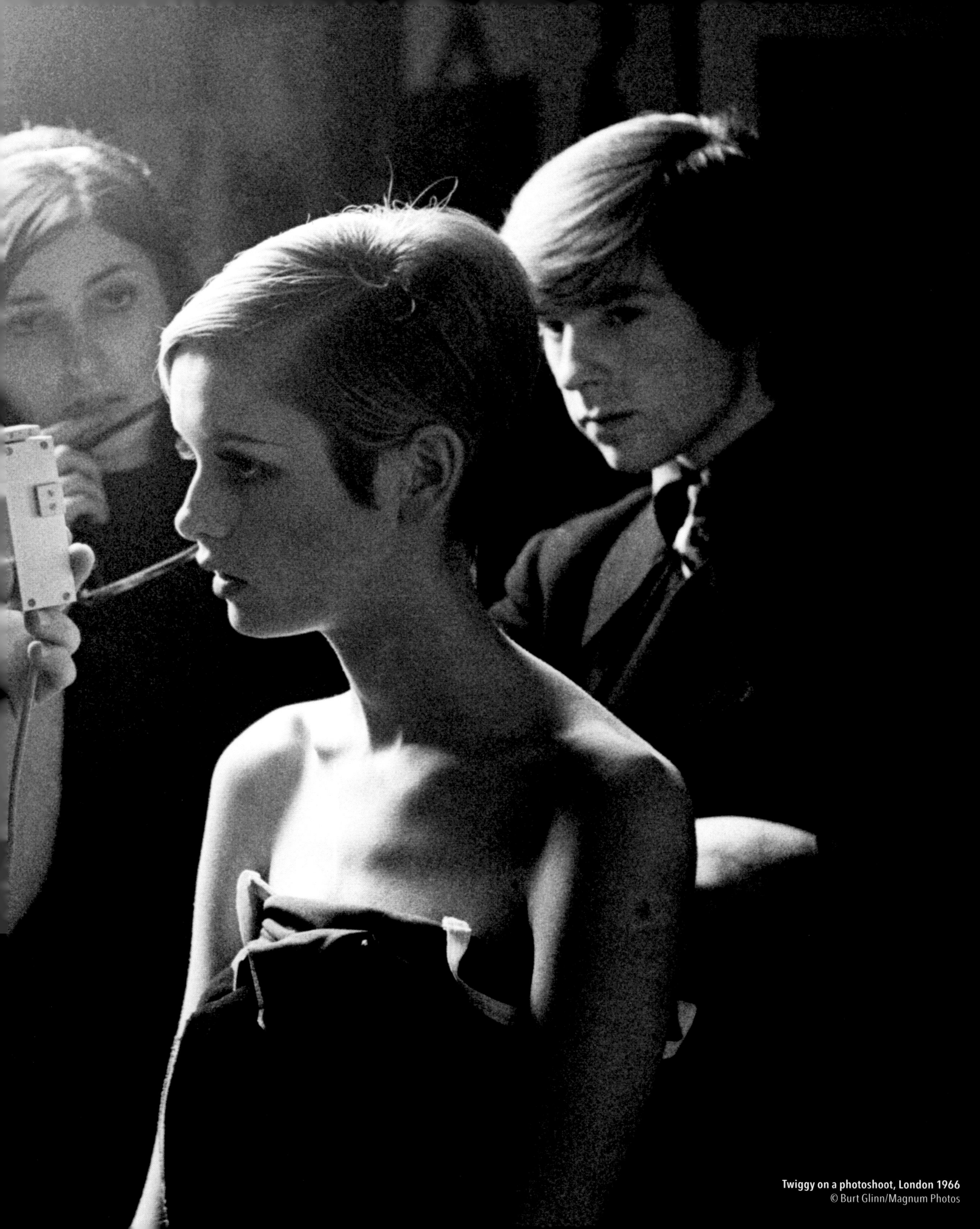

Twiggy on a photoshoot, London 1966
© Burt Glinn/Magnum Photos

Alek Wek

Seeing Alek Wek for the first time felt like seeing an oasis in a desert. I
spent so many years as a child feeling and believing that my night-shaded
skin barred me from this ephemeral thing known as "beauty." And then
I saw Alek Wek! And there was no doubt of her blackness, her darkness,
or her beauty. Suddenly I had a mirror of hope to hold up against myself,
a way of seeing or aspiring to be someone in this world who radiated grace,
composure, and elegance. It's difficult to know what's possible if we don't
see a version of ourselves in the world. I'm so grateful for Alek and the af-
firmation she sent to me, that beauty comes in all shades, and even on the
days you don't believe in yourself, there is someone in the world holding up
a mirror to show you how valuable your life can be.

Lupita Nyong'o

Photography by Steven Meisel

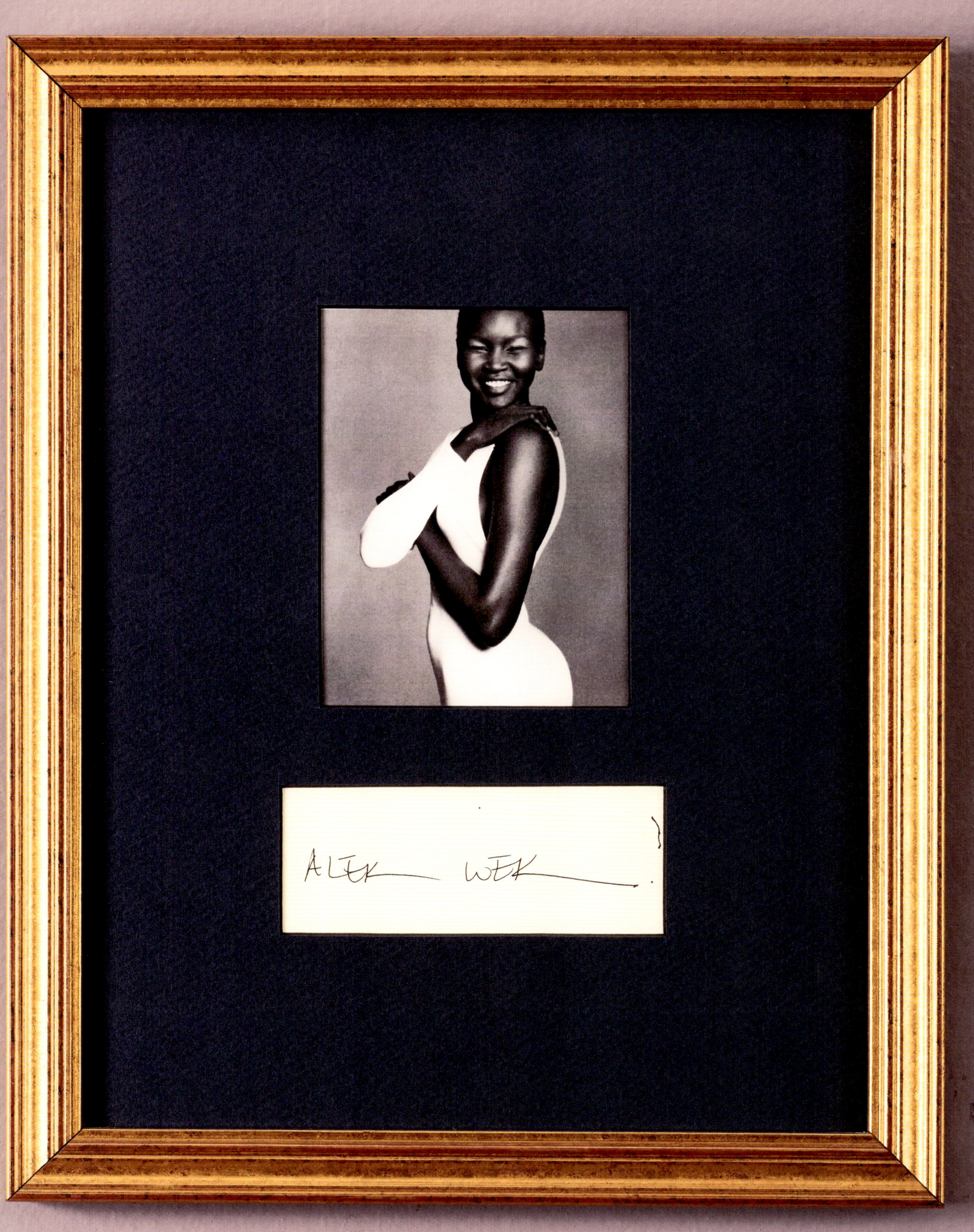

Jerry Hall

The first thing one notices when one sees Jerry is her long, gorgeous blonde hair, her big bright smile, and her determined Texan attitude. Being a Texan girl myself, I appreciate that can-do spirit. Modeling on the runways of the world, she was always special, not because of the clothing but because of her great personality. Our times together have always been filled with sincere respect for each other. When she walked hand in hand with her new husband, Rupert Murdoch, the huge smiles on both their faces said it all. I wish my dear friend happiness always.

Lynn Wyatt

Photography by Antonio Lopez

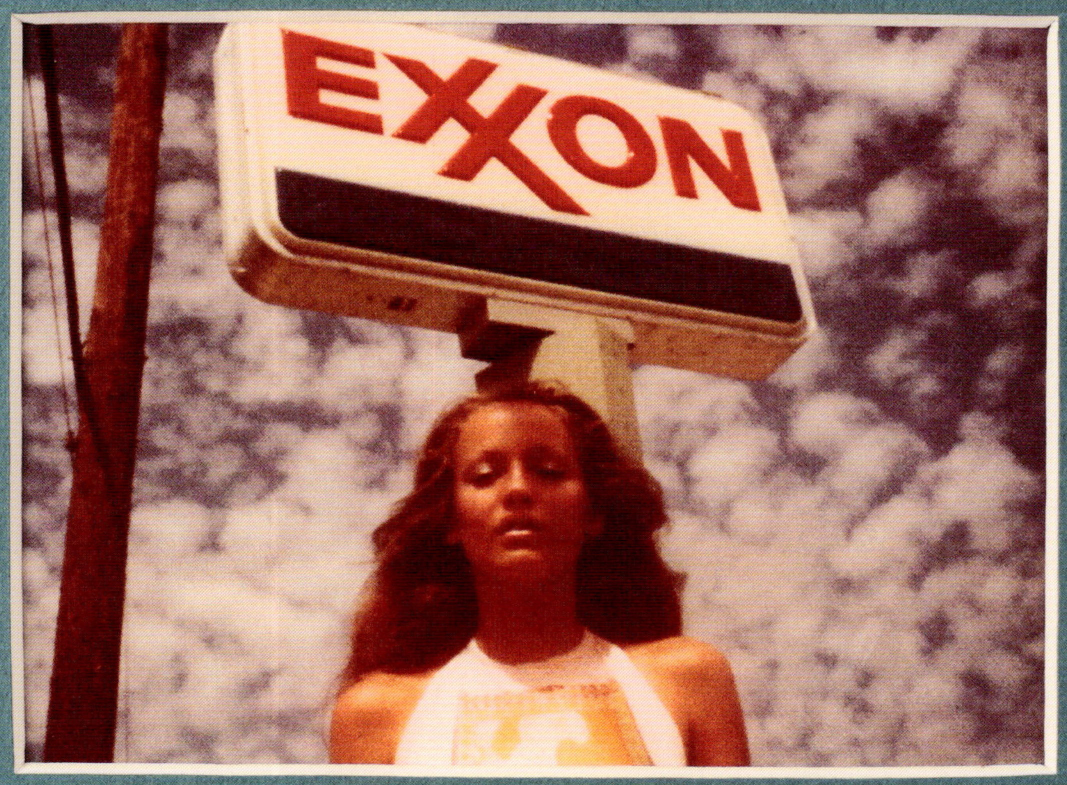

EXXON

Amanda Lear

I once heard Amanda Lear reminiscing about her time as a starving art student in Paris in the early 1960s, when she was scouted by Anita Pallenberg's agent: "You're so skin-and-bones, it's marvelous! Let me put you to work." So Amanda, five foot ten, 34–25–36, "blondette" with dark almond eyes, became a model specializing in hair, legs, and lingerie. What Salvador Dali, her genius Pygmalion for almost two decades, adored most, though, was "her skull." She modeled for YSL, Ossie Clarke, and Mary Quant, and was shot for Vogue and *Elle* by the likes of Helmut Newton.

But Amanda resented being simply a "smiling hanger" in Swinging London and Yé-yé Paris, so she learned how to run the show. Piling up the legendary lovers—Brian Jones, Brian Ferry, David Bowie—the pretty young thing built up a pre-Kardashian machinery: album cover muse, pop singer, TV personality, gay icon, thespian, comic character, intellectuals' favorite confidante... all spiced with the transgender rumor that, nowadays, carries a perfect, edgy chic.

For forty years now, she's been playing that bad-ass, hilarious, unsinkable vamp. Her wisdom seems to come from the mix of fashion and surrealism she was raised on. Performance doesn't hide truth. Truth itself is a joke.

Carole Sabas

Photography by Unknown

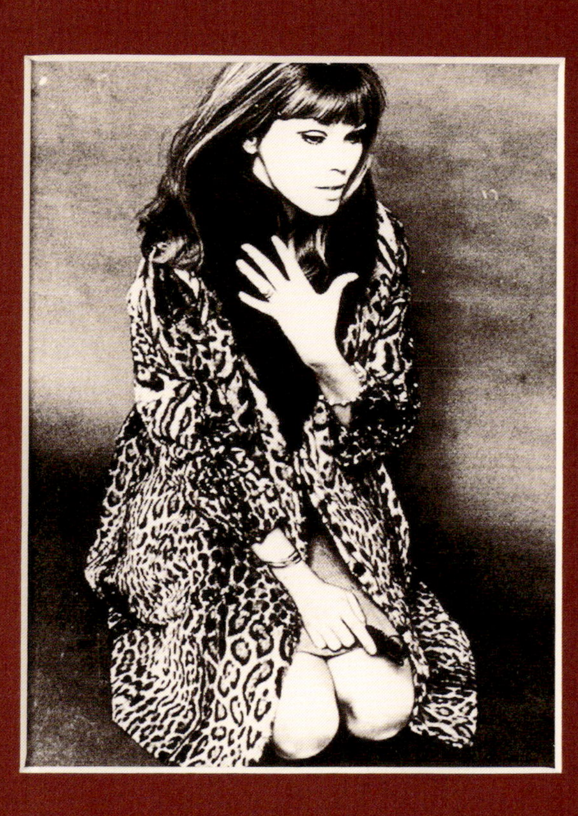

Thinking about Cindy Crawford fills me with memories of being a teenager in the 1990s in Toledo, Ohio, looking from the outside at a glamorous, untouchable superworld. Cindy Crawford was not just a part of that world; she was one of its creators and inspirations. Yet, when I saw her in *House of Style* on MTV, she seemed… just, really nice. High fashion, music, and television were somehow, suddenly, not so far away. I felt pride that a girl with brown hair, like mine, could become a cultural icon.

Cindy not only changed the perception of "sexy American girl" from the classic blue-eyed blonde to a funny, smart, charming brunette; she also gave us an image of a strong, athletic, empowered woman in charge of her sex appeal. She was valedictorian of her high school class, and got a college scholarship to study chemical engineering. She taught me that beauty is not separate from intelligence—that, in fact, glamour and sex appeal are strengthened by and intertwined with a woman's intelligence. In my opinion, it was Cindy's strength and wisdom that created the concept of the supermodel.

To me, she is a superwoman. Whatever she does, she rises to the top: her magazine covers, which continue to influence the direction of covers today; her iconic appearance in George Michael's "Freedom 90" video; her memorable Pepsi ad; her workout videos, furniture line, skin care line, and charity efforts. I am thankful to have been inspired by her in my formative years, and I continue to be influenced by her as a mother and a businesswoman.

Katie Holmes

Photography by Irving Penn

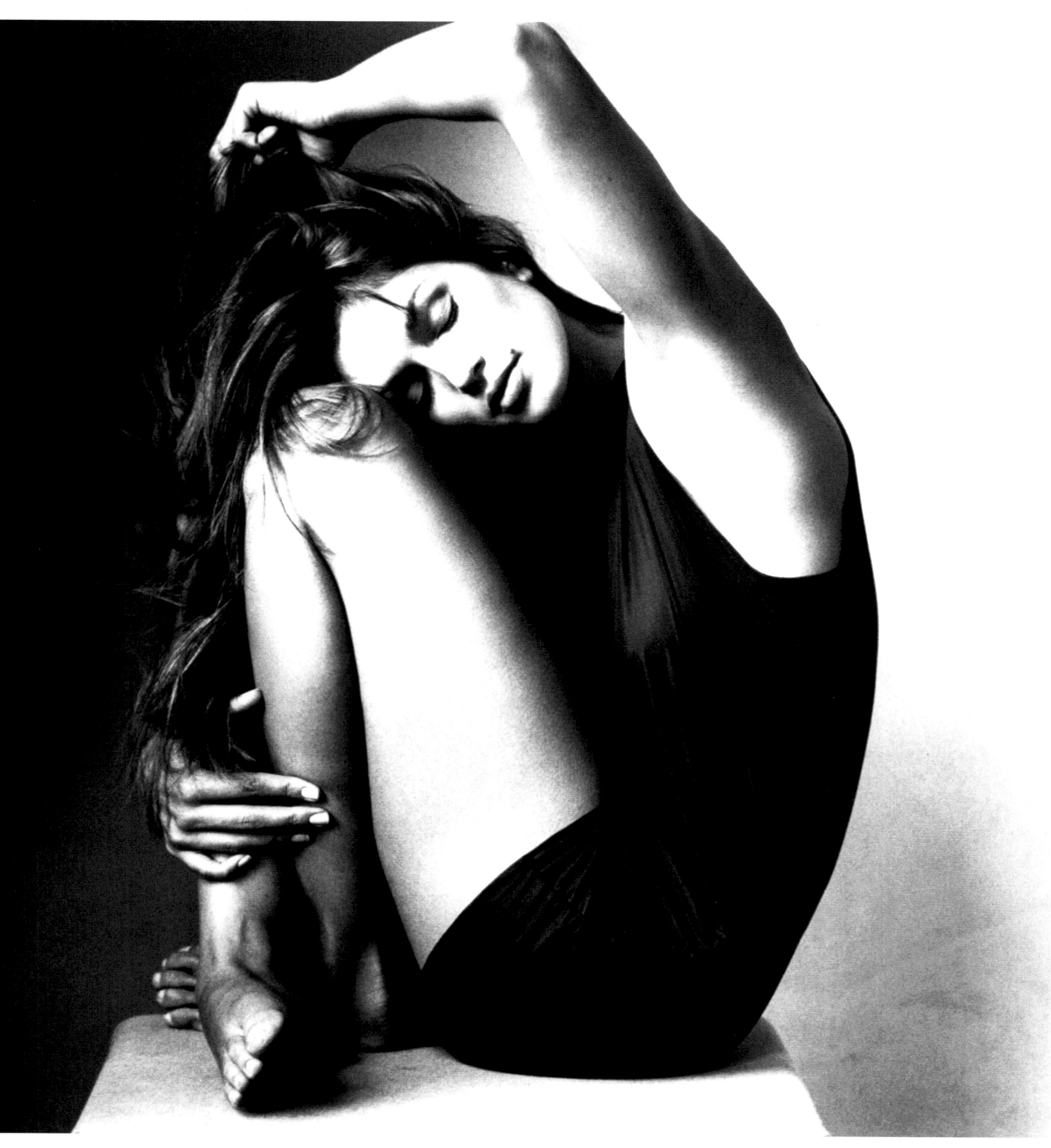

Marisa Berenson

I met Marisa in 1965. She was seventeen, about to turn eighteen. I was eighteen. In those days, we used to swan around the Central Park fountain on Sundays. The scene was social and the looks were haute hippie and real hippies. Think *Hair* the musical, and the parade of divine creatures of that time. Think Vreeland *Vogue*, but in real life. The looks went from day to evening and back again. Baroque, bohemian, bedazzled.

In 1970, Marisa and I reunited and became close friends. The walls of her apartment on 57th Street were covered in blue, black, and white fabric. It was like walking into a divine Chinese vase. She was on multiple *Vogue* covers at the time, and was a muse and great friend of Yves Saint Laurent, Halston, Valentino, Giorgio di Sant' Angelo, and Fernando Sanchez, all of whom mixed with one another in an inspiring, inspired time. She was on the cover of *Newsweek* with the tagline "Queen of the Scene."

I first did a portrait of Marisa in 1971 for Halston, who commissioned me to draw many of his favorite women. Marisa had introduced me to him at her sister Berry's loft on Second Avenue. Marisa also asked me to draw her, as a gift to Helmut Berger. Later, in the early 1990s, I did many photographs of her in New York and in Southampton. Daytime, nighttime, great times. Haute and hot. Like Marisa.

In her modeling images, Marisa manages to be exciting, calm, and sexy. Very. In her movie roles the same qualities are there, but the motion picture camera interprets that energy in a magnified way. Marisa exudes a powerful stillness. You either got it or you don't. And boy, has she got it!

Marisa's beauty is the first thing one sees, then and now, and it makes a powerful first impression. Quickly, it is eclipsed by her great poise and kindness. Unique, then and now—inside, outside, all sides. I love her.

David Croland

Photography by Hulton Archive

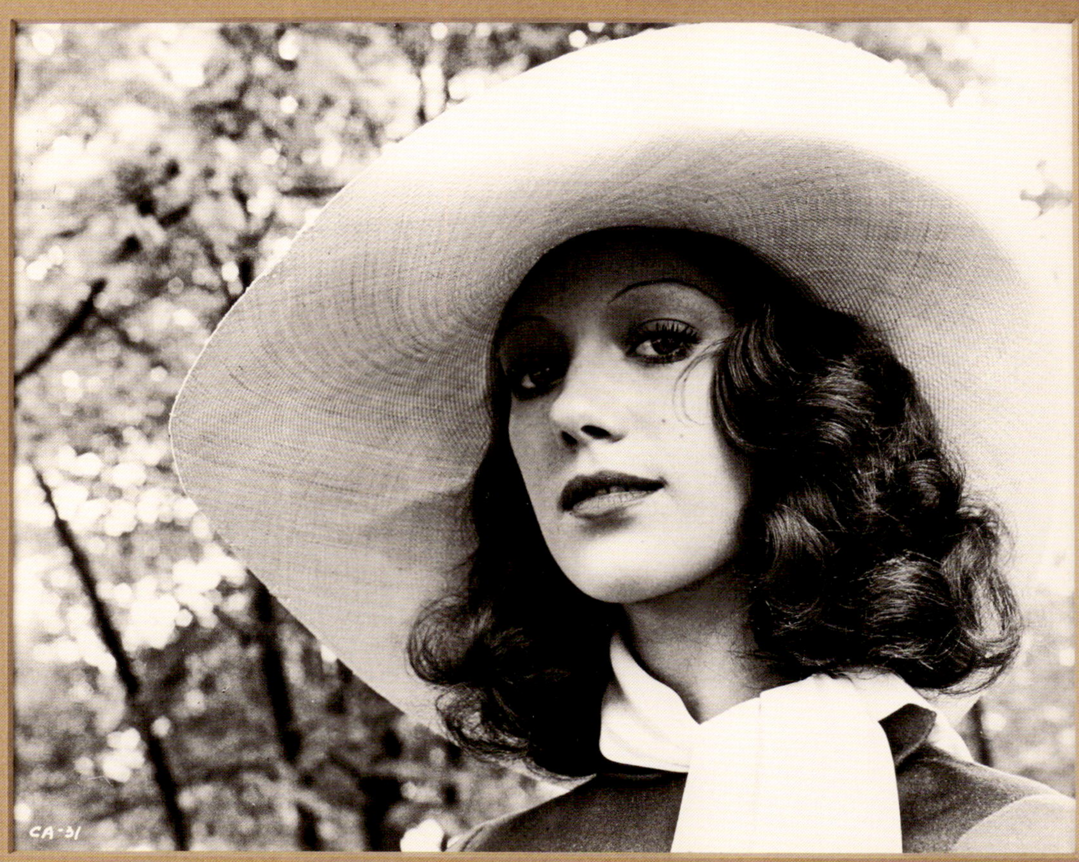

Grace Coddington

In 1964, when I was still pretty fresh on the scene, I was asked to shoot the new Vidal Sassoon "Five Points" haircut for *Queen* magazine. The model was Grace Coddington, whom I was shooting at least once a week at the time. She was always soft-spoken and easy to get on with, and she was a natural model in clothing. It seemed like she didn't have to do anything at all.

The fashion editor was Lady Clare Rendlesham, a legend in her own lunchtime, and she was not happy. She came to my studio, picked up the phone, and screamed, "Why can't I have David Bailey!" That filled me with confidence... not!

The shoot went fine, but when I came to develop the film, my nerves got the better of me. Somehow I overdeveloped it, making it a harsh, steely black and white with no midtones. All that was left were the five points the haircut had been named after, and the profile of Grace's elegant nose. The picture made history, but the truth is, it was just one big accident.

David Montgomery

Photography by Terence Donovan

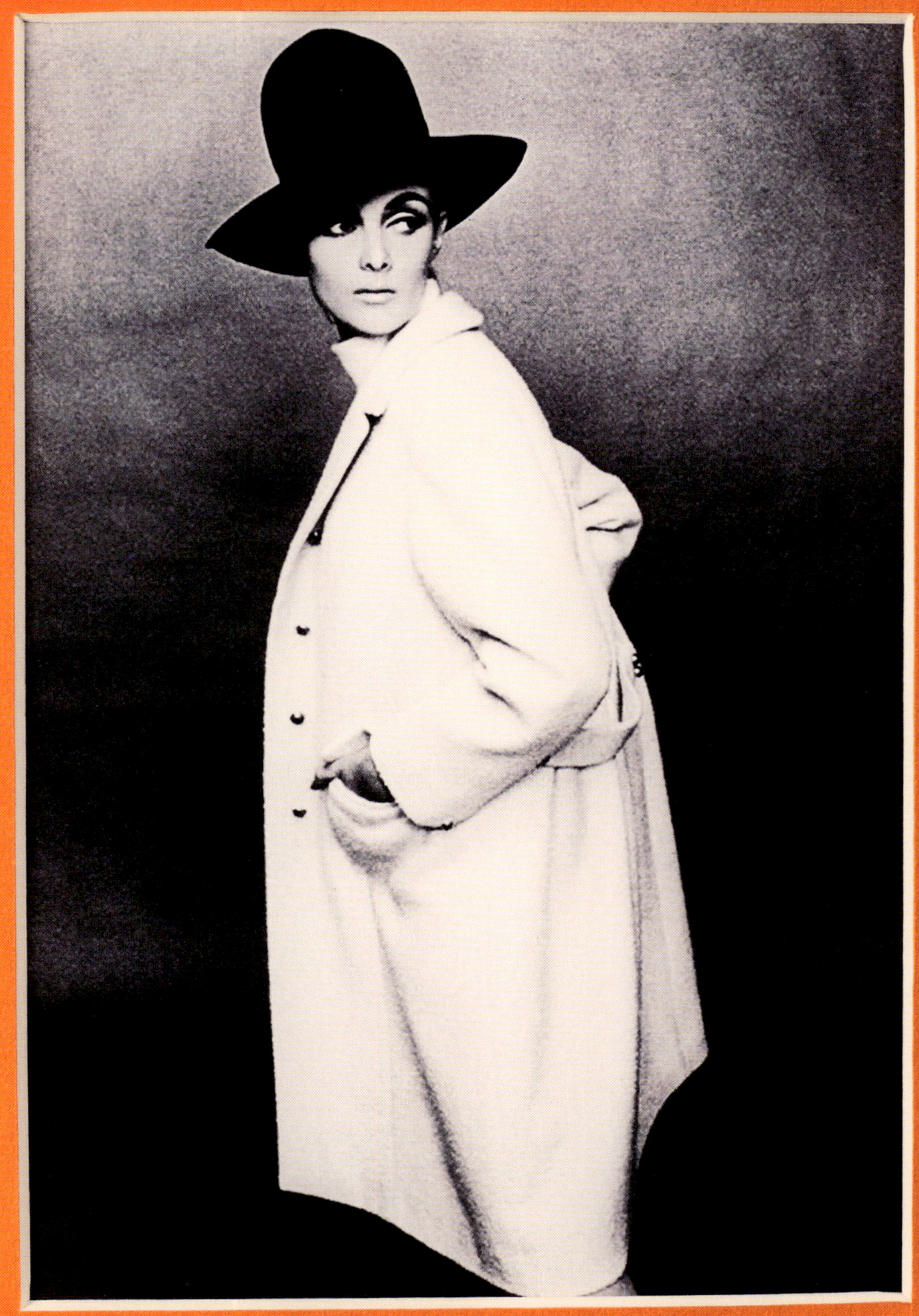

Lauren Hutton

Lauren Hutton is a Voltaire-quoting Tulane grad, who didn't have her
teeth fixed, didn't have drastic plastic surgery, and didn't see marrying
a plutocrat as the ultimate career move. Like many would-be models,
she spent time as a bunny at the Playboy Club, but she is one of the rare
few who became an actress and didn't embarrass herself. She traveled
Africa, smoked cigars in the Himalayas, and wrestled alligators for
Helmut Newton. She made Armani cool. When Hutton got older, she
wore her age proudly, and designers like Tomas Maier and Alexis Bittar
hired her to do campaigns and appear in their fashion shows. Which is
fitting, because like their brands, she is classic, expensive, and cool.

Jacob Bernstein

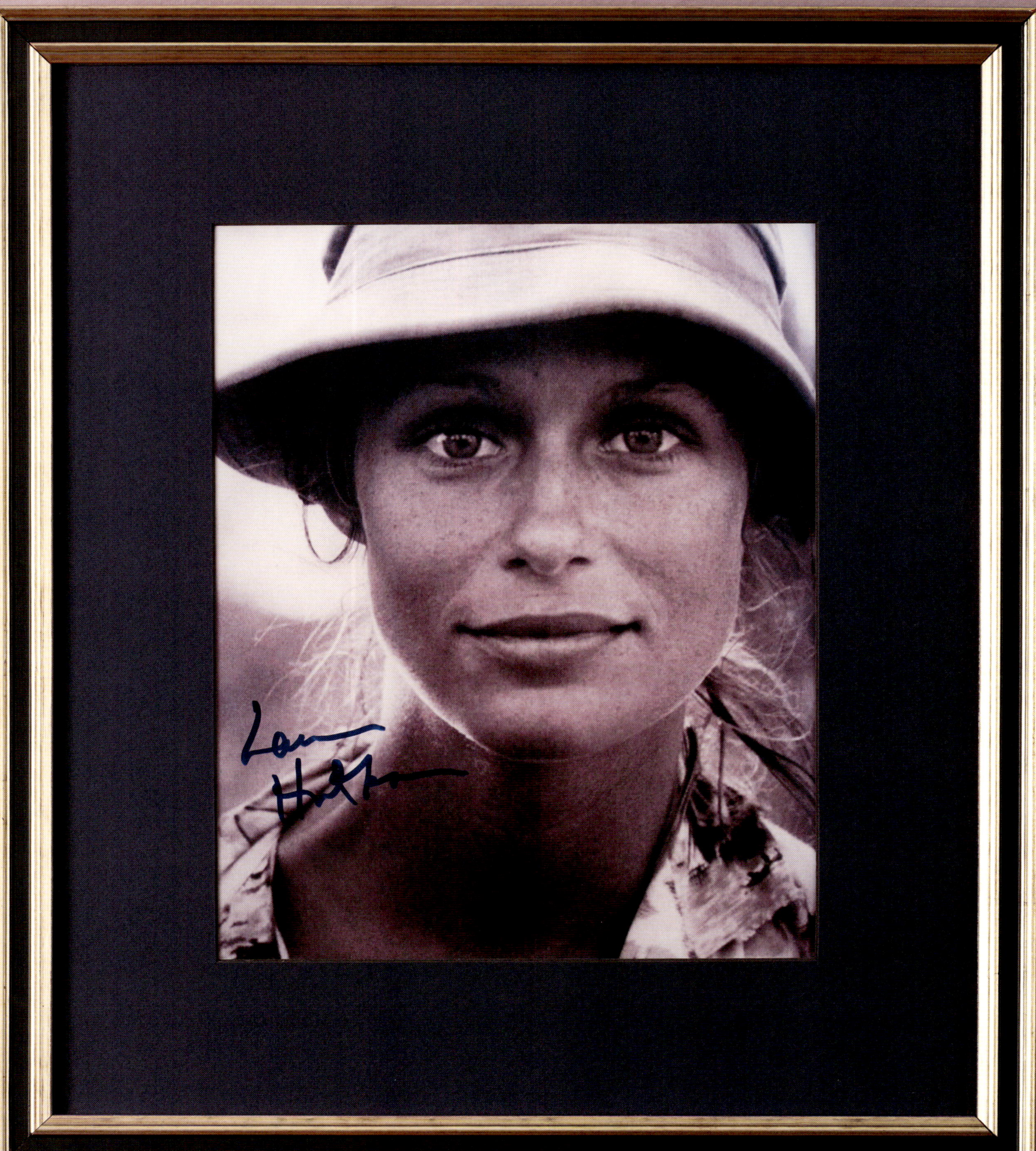

In 1947, aged sixteen, Carmen Dell'Orefice became *Vogue*'s youngest ever cover girl. In 2008, the *Guinness Book of World Records* declared hers to be the longest career in modeling history. As I write this, she is lighting up Times Square in the Christmas campaign for H & M. Now in her ninth decade, she has endured and ultimately triumphed in an industry that can still be made nervous by thirty-year-olds. Among the era-defining photographers who recorded her evolution from shy, skinny teenager to all-American pinup to high-fashion swan were Cecil Beaton, Richard Avedon, Horst P. Horst, and Irving Penn. After a hiatus, she returned as a soignée and still sexy fifty-, sixty-, seventy-, and eighty-year-old. Along the way, she posed for Salvador Dali, modeled hats with Marilyn Monroe, made cameo appearances in films by Martin Scorsese and Woody Allen, and twice lost her savings—most recently to Bernard Madoff. Through it all, she has kept her equilibrium and her humor. "I was never an It girl," she says. "I was a silent actress"—but no Norma Desmond. Carmen, as ever, has her eye on the future. She is planning for one hundred: "After that, I may slow down." It's not that she has discovered the fountain of youth; she wasn't looking for it. Sorceress that she is, she has found a way to turn years into assets.

David Downton

Photography by Richard Avedon

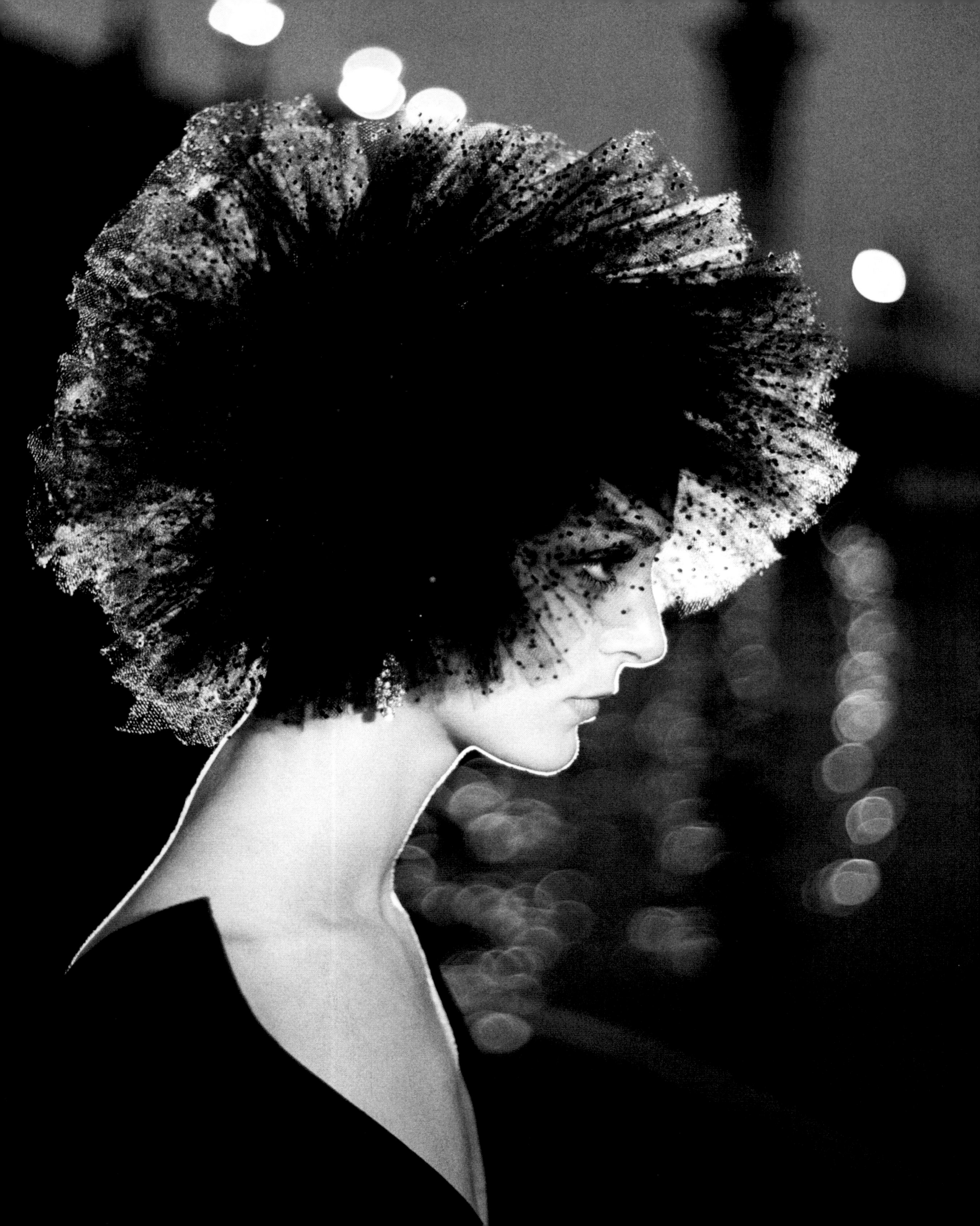

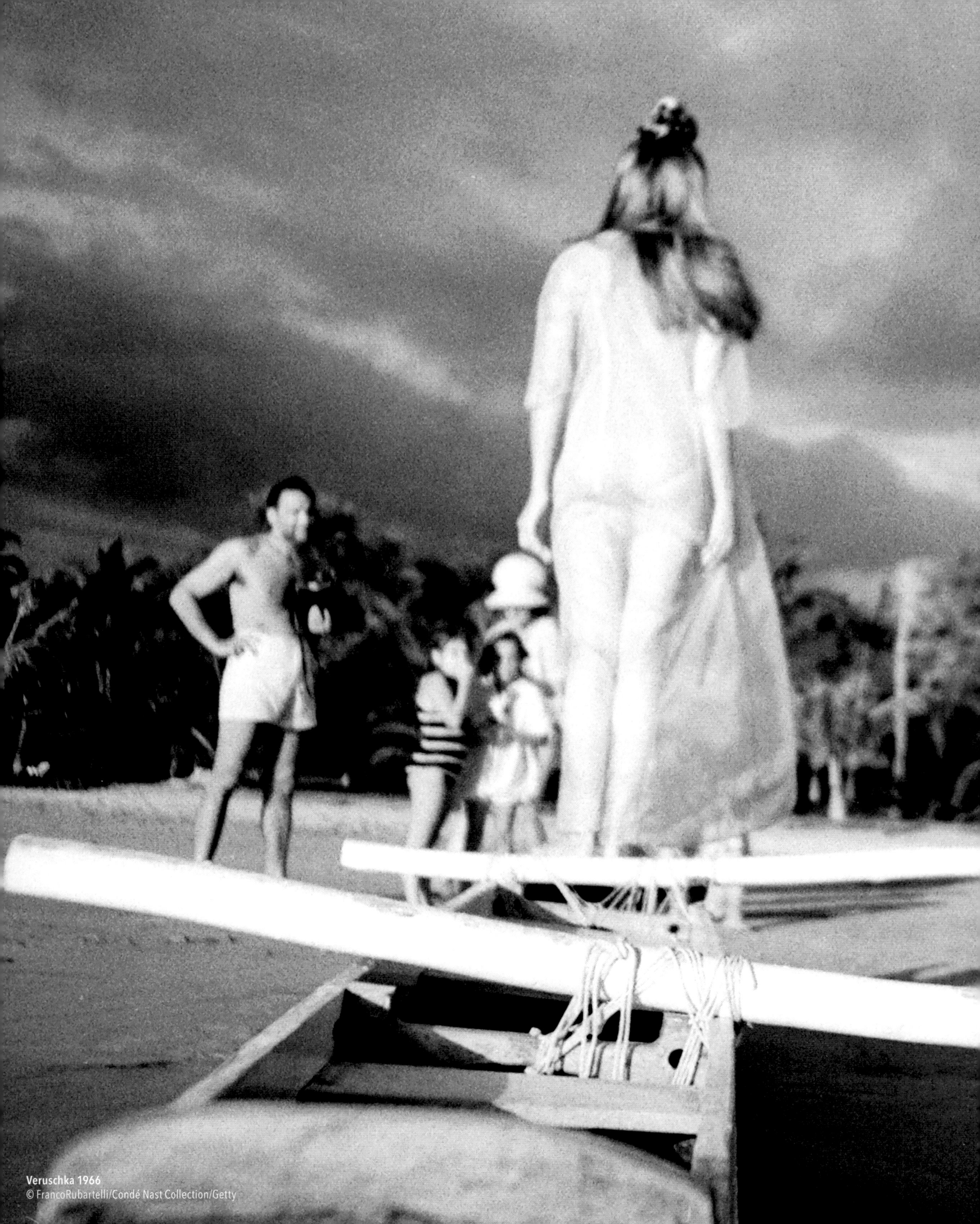

Veruschka 1966

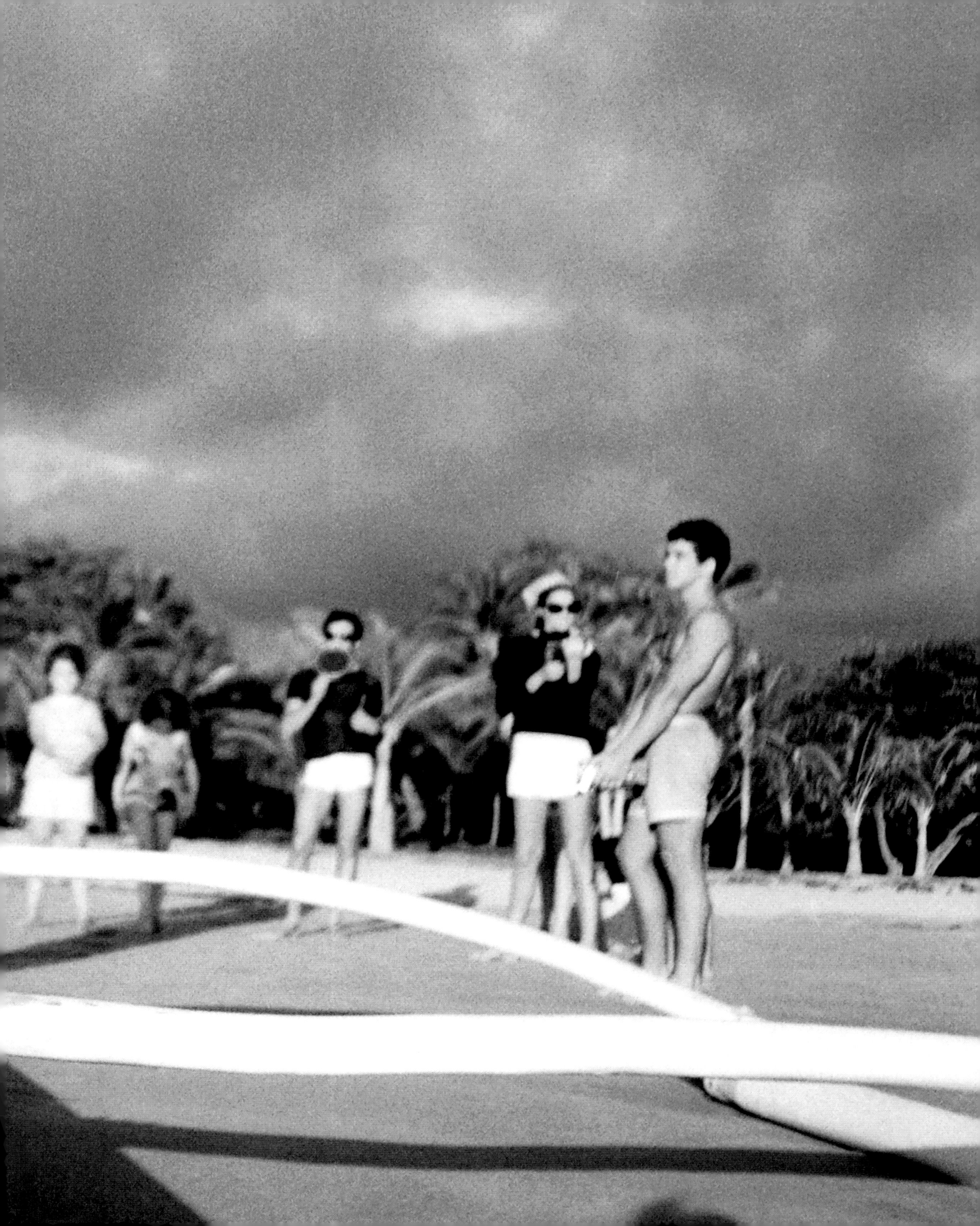

Anyone who knows me knows that fashion's not exactly my forte, so I surround myself with people who make me look good. For over fifteen seasons, I've been lucky enough to work with Heidi on *Project Runway*. Heidi's truly got a sparkle in her eye, and behind that sparkle is one of the most hardworking, fun-loving individuals I know. I'm amazed by her boundless energy. Her love of life is inspiring. She is a go-getter and willing to put in the time to elevate any project, on or off the runway. Her incredible work ethic is what's responsible for her many accomplishments—supermodel, actress, TV host, businesswoman. I've seen Heidi grow into a multi-hyphenate over the years, and I couldn't be more proud of her—and besides that, she's one terrific friend.

To steal a phrase from *Project Runway*, in my opinion Heidi will always be "in."

Harvey Weinstein

Photography by Steven Meisel

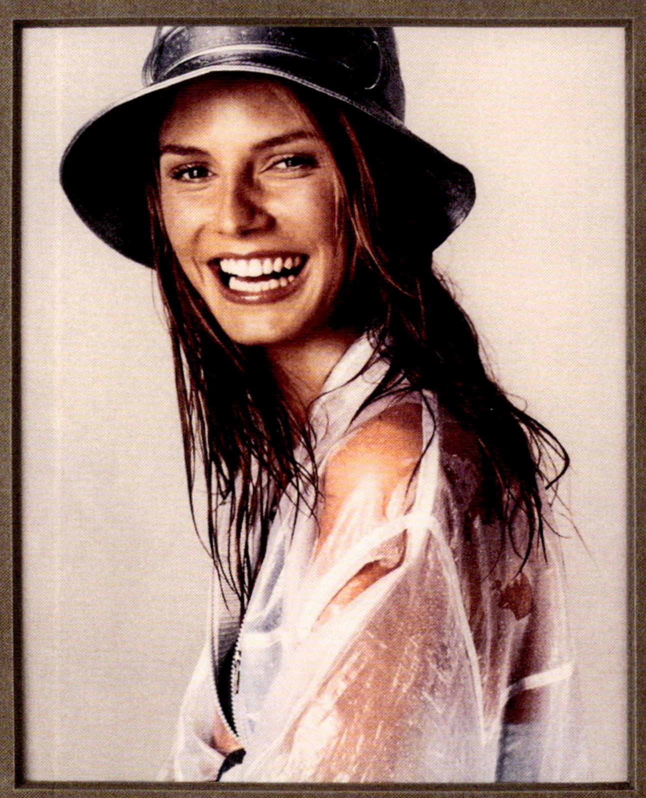

Heidi Klum

Iman

Iman's legacy is undisputed: as Yves Saint Laurent's muse, as Michael Jackson's video girl, or as an icon of the 1970s' New York disco scene. With her timeless beauty, her distinctive and regal East African features, she was one of the first models to redefine the idea of black beauty in the fashion industry. She opened doors for many models of color to follow.

Most importantly, Iman used her early experience in fashion, when it was hard to find cosmetics suitable for her skin tone, to develop and launch a successful global cosmetics brand for all ethnicities. She transformed a personal need into a million-dollar business that to this day remains unique in a beauty industry obsessed with sameness.

Edward Enninful

Photography by Scavullo

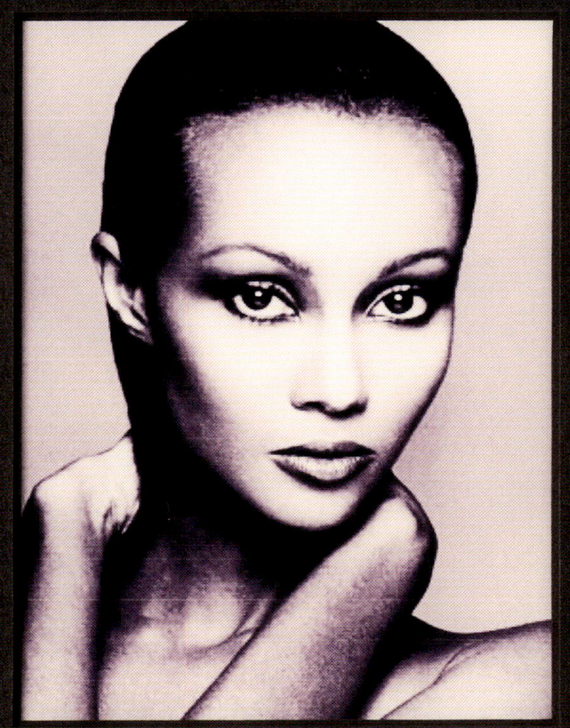

Love
2011

Apollonia van Ravenstein

Apollonia has an aristocratic sense that allows her to transform into whatever style she wears.

Luxury with her is always high. Her photos are what Umberto Eco called *opere aperte*—open works—that change according to the eye of the beholder.

Gian Paolo Barbieri

Photography by Gian Paolo Barbieri

VOGUE

ITALIA

MODA:

UOVO
LASSICO
I TRE
SSI
EL PRÊT-
-PORTER:
AINT
AURENT
NGARO
NDRE'
AUG

OSA C'E'
I NUOVO
OTTO
SOLE
ER LA
OSTRA

BELLEZZA

N PARADISO
CONOSCIUTO
ER LE

VACANZE:
E ISOLE
EYCHELLES

Apollonia

Marie was one of the big stars of Saint Laurent's most glorious period.
She broke the barriers for Asian girls in the Seventies. Such a beauty!

Manolo Blahnik

Photography by David Bailey

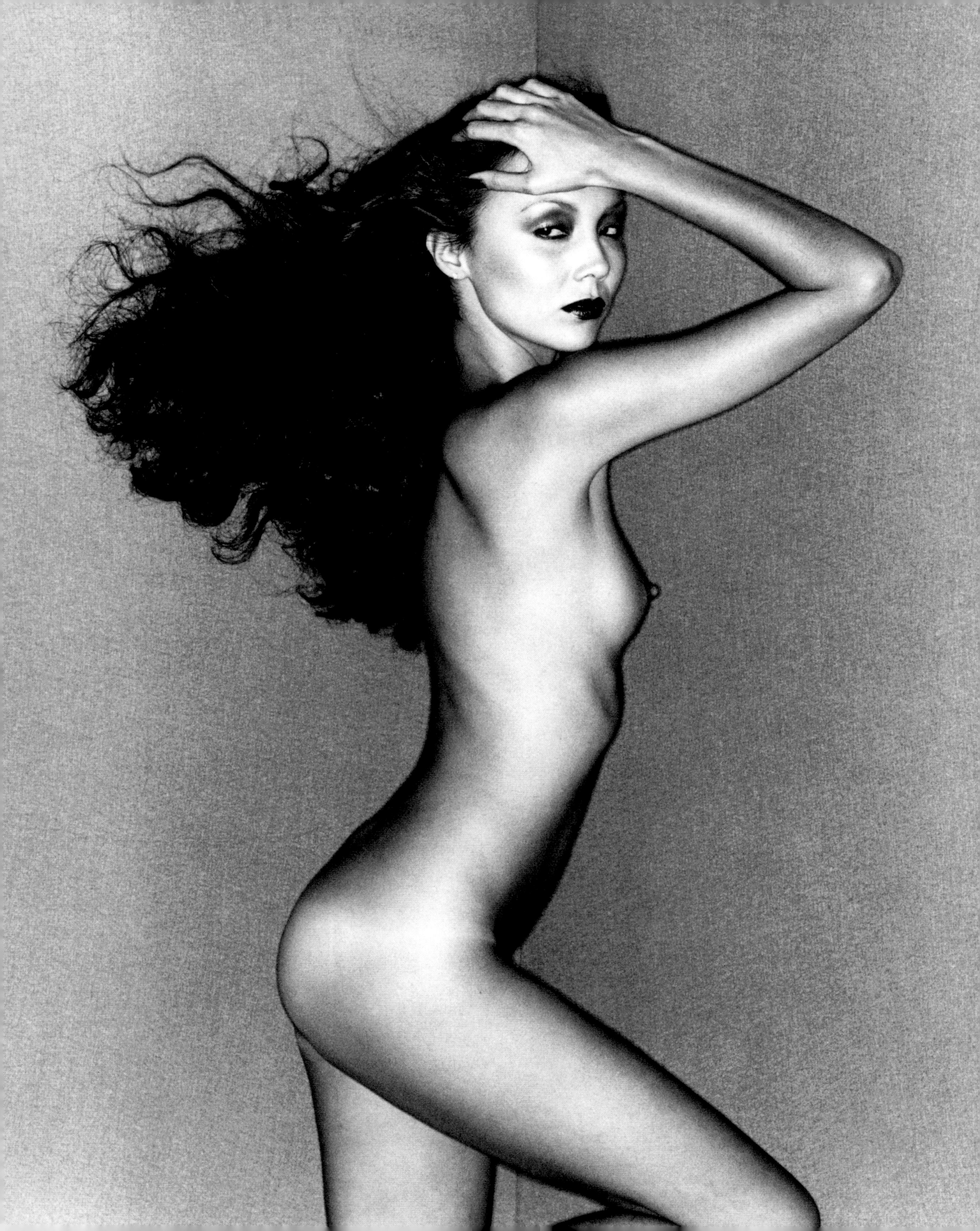

Donna contains multitudes.

She is the gender-bending partner of Stella Tennant and Kate Moss in the Warholian Calvin Klein perfume ads shot by Steven Meisel. The virgin from outer space in Hiro's hypnotic photographs for *Harper's Bazaar*. The backpacking hippie on the verge of a nervous breakdown in Bob Richardson's masterpiece portfolio for Paris *Vogue*. The energetic clotheshorse jumping against a white background for Avedon and Diana Vreeland. The innocent dollybird in ringlets and Victorian lace looking defiantly into the camera of David Bailey. The *grande dame* wrapped in furs in the back of a chauffeur-driven car in Jean-Loup Sieff's Visconti-like drama.

All roads lead to Donna.

Christopher Niquet

Photography by Hiro

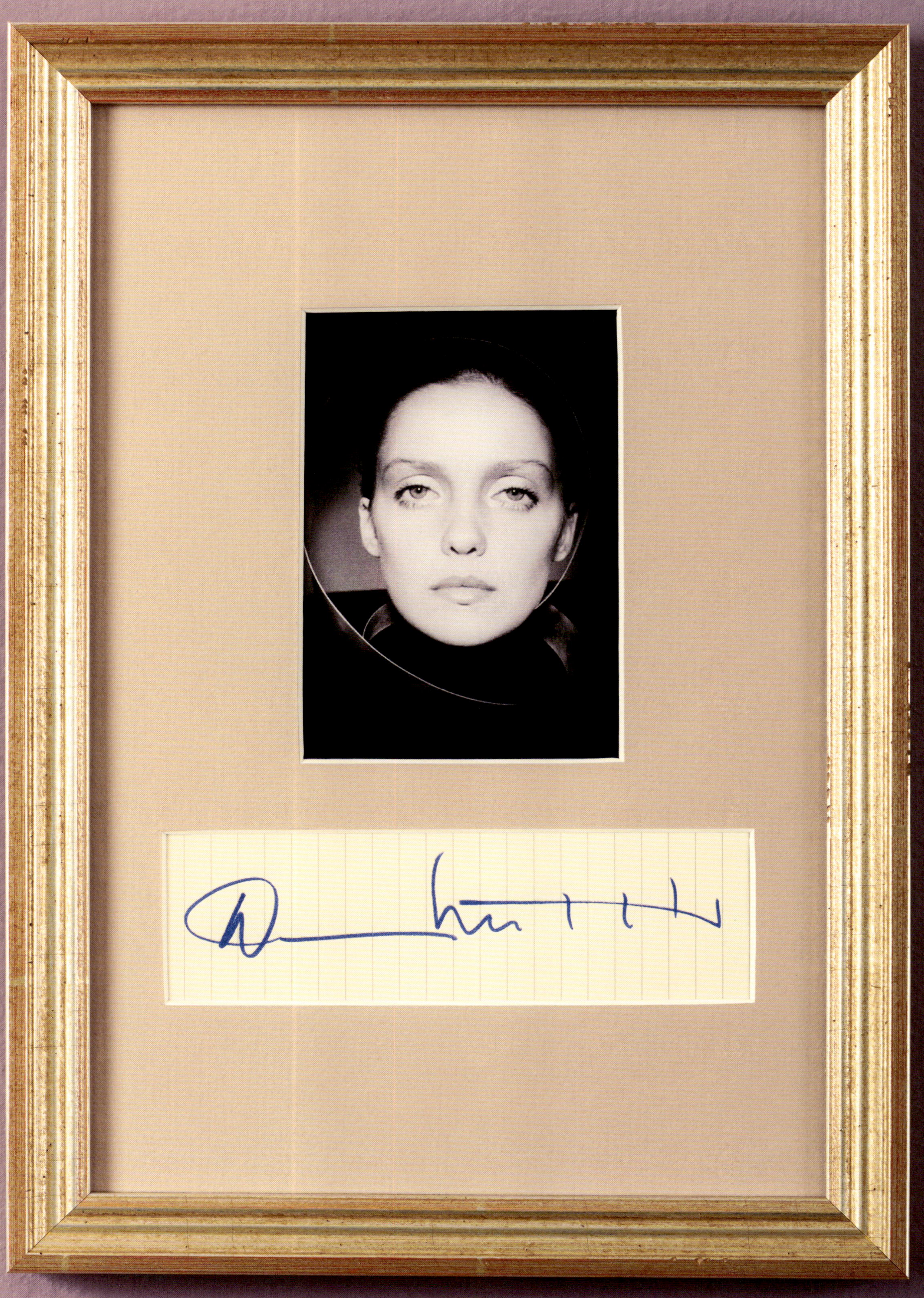

How could I not want to write about Brooke Shields? When you look back at the fashion and film of the 1980s, her name stands out. By taking on movie roles and ad campaigns that others might have shied away from, and doing them tastefully, Brooke helped redefine and reshape what it meant to be beautiful and talented—not just in America, but the world over.

But Brooke is much more than a pretty face. She is a loving mother and a smart, beautiful woman who has used her name and platform to bring awareness to causes and issues including AIDS research, and has bravely shared her experience of postpartum depression. It isn't easy for child stars to transition into adulthood. But this kid turned out better than just all right. Bravo, Brooke!

Cornelia Guest

Photography by Unknown

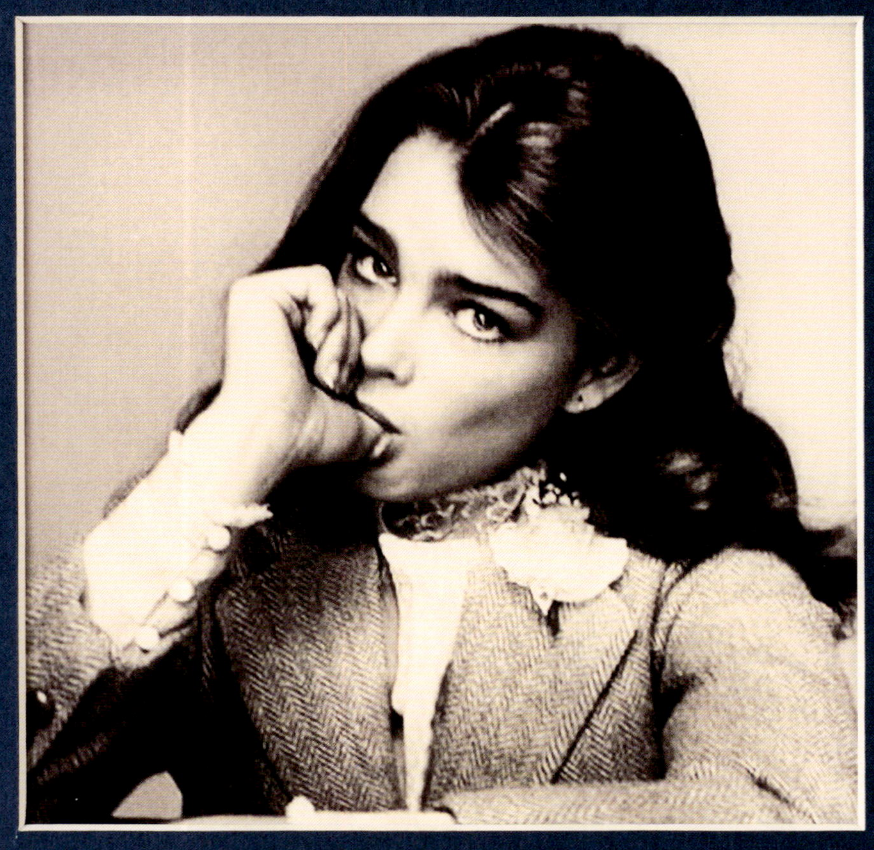

Oh my!,
Merci! & Thank you!,
love,
Brooke Shields

When I first heard her name, Guinevere, a singular world took shape in my mind: one suffused by medieval legend.

When I met her, my imagination ran wild. I was struck by her grace, the peculiar beauty of her skin, her delicacy... By her unique presence, her insouciant detachment. She had a tender look in her eyes that suggested a dry sense of humor and an offbeat intellect.

Soon after that, Craig McDean and I created a "visual novel" for Jil Sander's Summer 1996 collection, with Guinevere—unique and immutably modern—at its center. Her personality was our inspiration. She inspires me still.

Marc Ascoli

Photography by Paolo Roversi

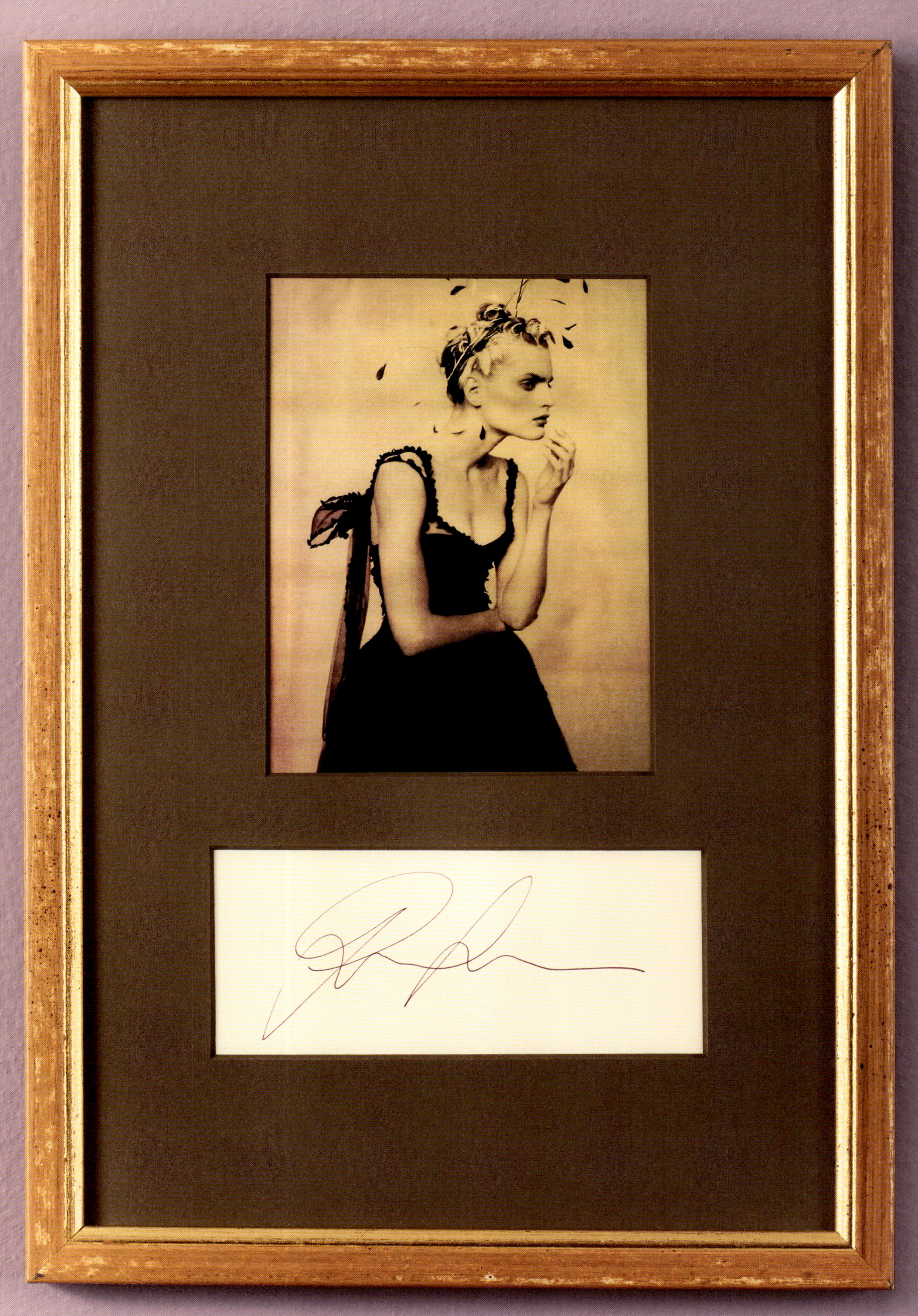

"Darling, we need some blue-blooded girls for Meisel," said Issie Blow, my boss at the time. "Can you find any?"

It was 1993, and I had just started working at British *Vogue* as Isabella Blow's assistant. She had a major project on her hands: a story by Steven Meisel, his first for the magazine. She had somehow persuaded him to cross the pond and photograph the coolest girls in London. Of course, Issie wanted them posh as well as cool. Provenance and style were everything to Issie.

After months of searching, and rejecting almost everyone she came across, Issie had decided on Honor Fraser and Bella Freud, among others. We had one spot left. I asked everyone I knew if they could suggest any aristocratic beauties for our story. One night a friend said to me, "Stella Tennant's really tall and model-y. But she's got a ring through her nose."

My interest was piqued. The Tennants were a famously bohemian, artistic Scottish family, much admired in society. I rang Stella and asked her to send her photo. In due course, a basic passport photo arrived of a gamine-looking girl with dark hair, enormous dark blue eyes and a pierced nose.

When Stella came into the *Vogue* offices, Issie immediately booked her for the Meisel shoot. Stella was very cool, very beautiful in an androgynous way, and couldn't have given a toss about being in a magazine. She had just left art school and was studying massage. I was rather in awe of her. It didn't hurt that her grandfather was the Duke of Devonshire—not that she'd *ever* have said anything. She was far too cool for that. The point was, she was the ultimate in posh, and the ultimate in cool.

There were endless discussions at the office about Stella's nose ring. The editor thought it was scary and didn't want her to wear it for the shoot. But Meisel and Issie were determined that it should stay where it was— and it did. A bit like Cindy Crawford's mole, that nose ring singled out Stella as having a different kind of beauty, one that was modern and right for the moment.

The "moment" that started for Stella on that photo shoot has lasted well over twenty years. She might not wear the nose ring any more, but no one has tired of looking at a woman who is still as edgy and chic as ever.

Plum Sykes

Photography by Steven Meisel

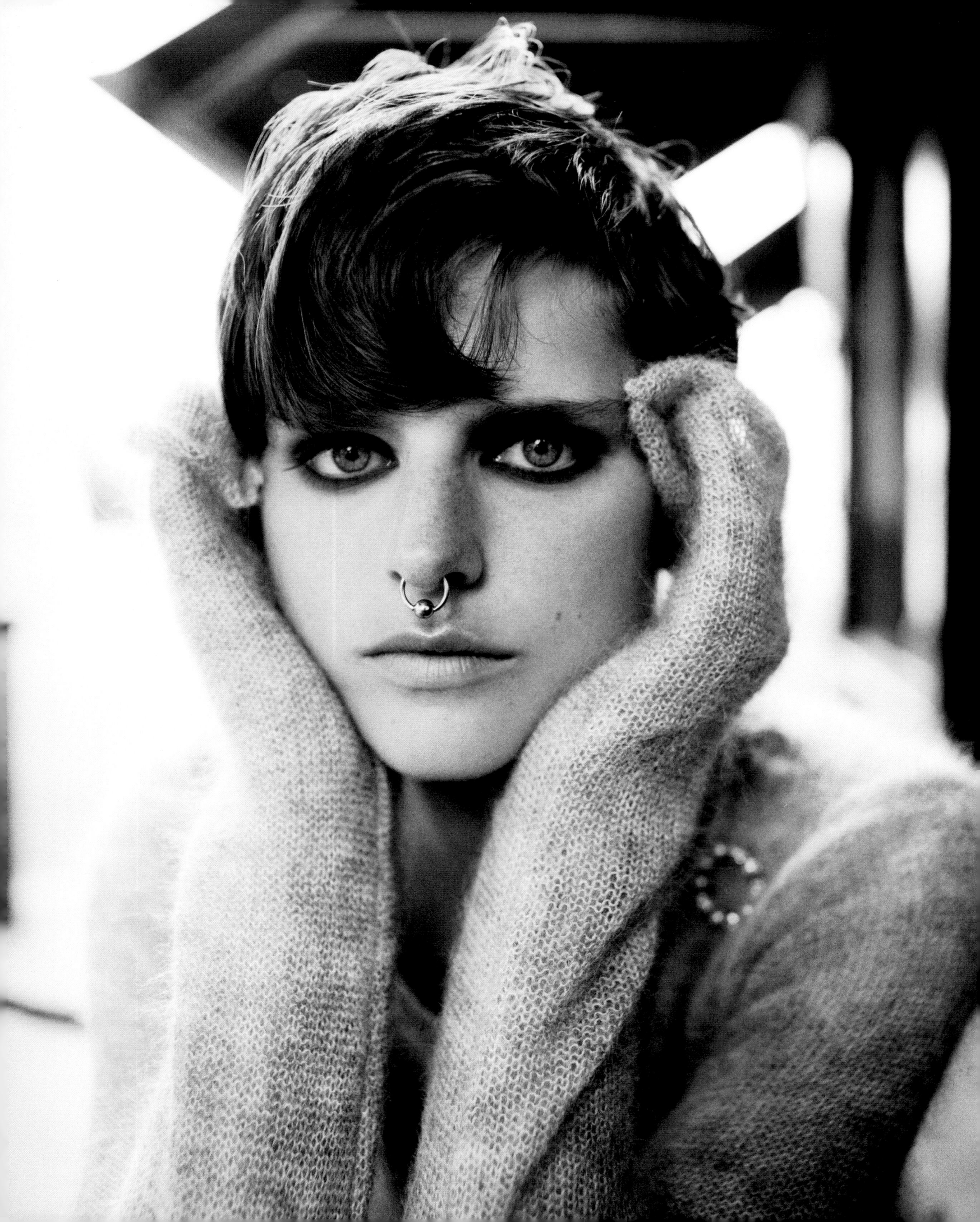

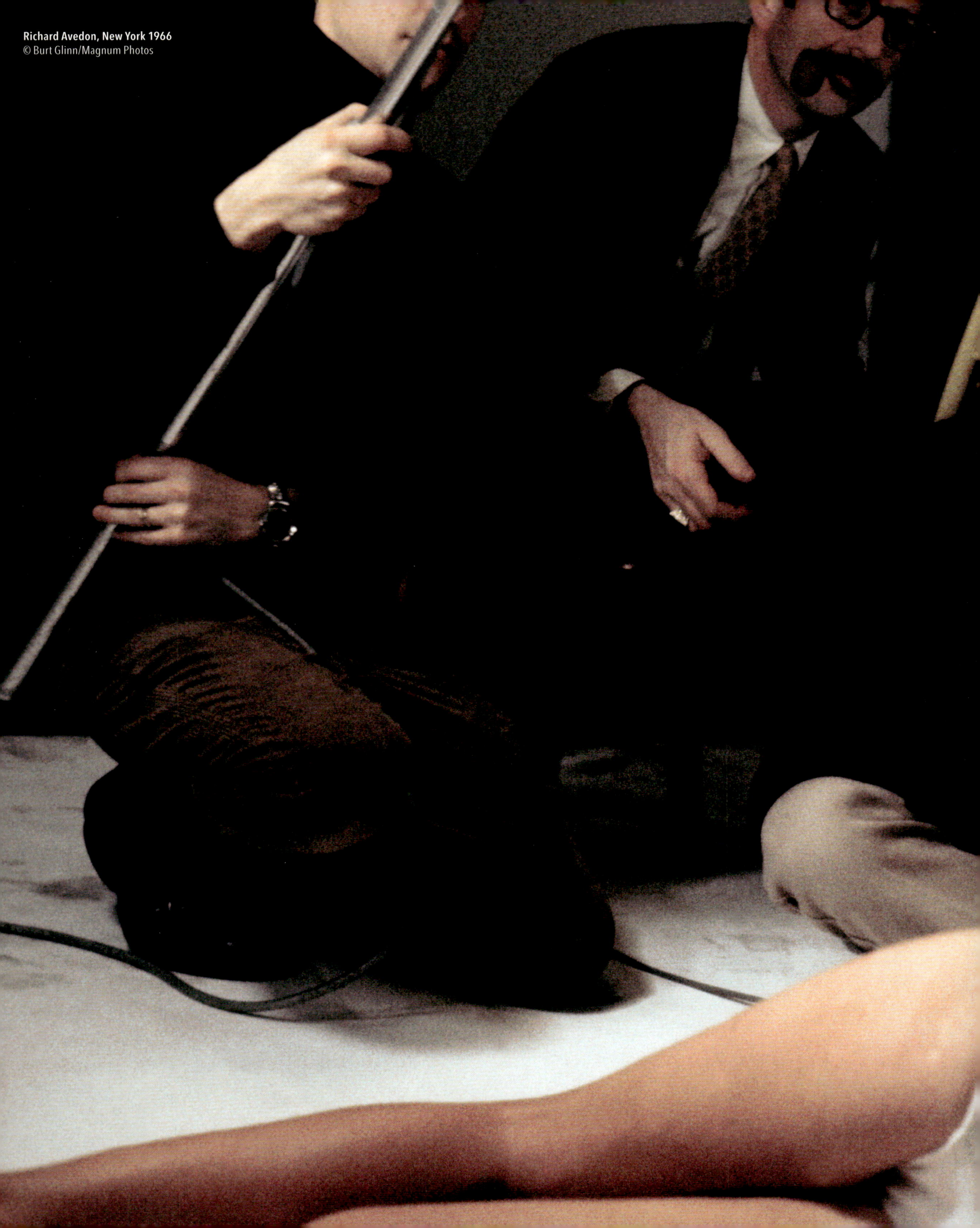

Richard Avedon, New York 1966
© Burt Glinn/Magnum Photos

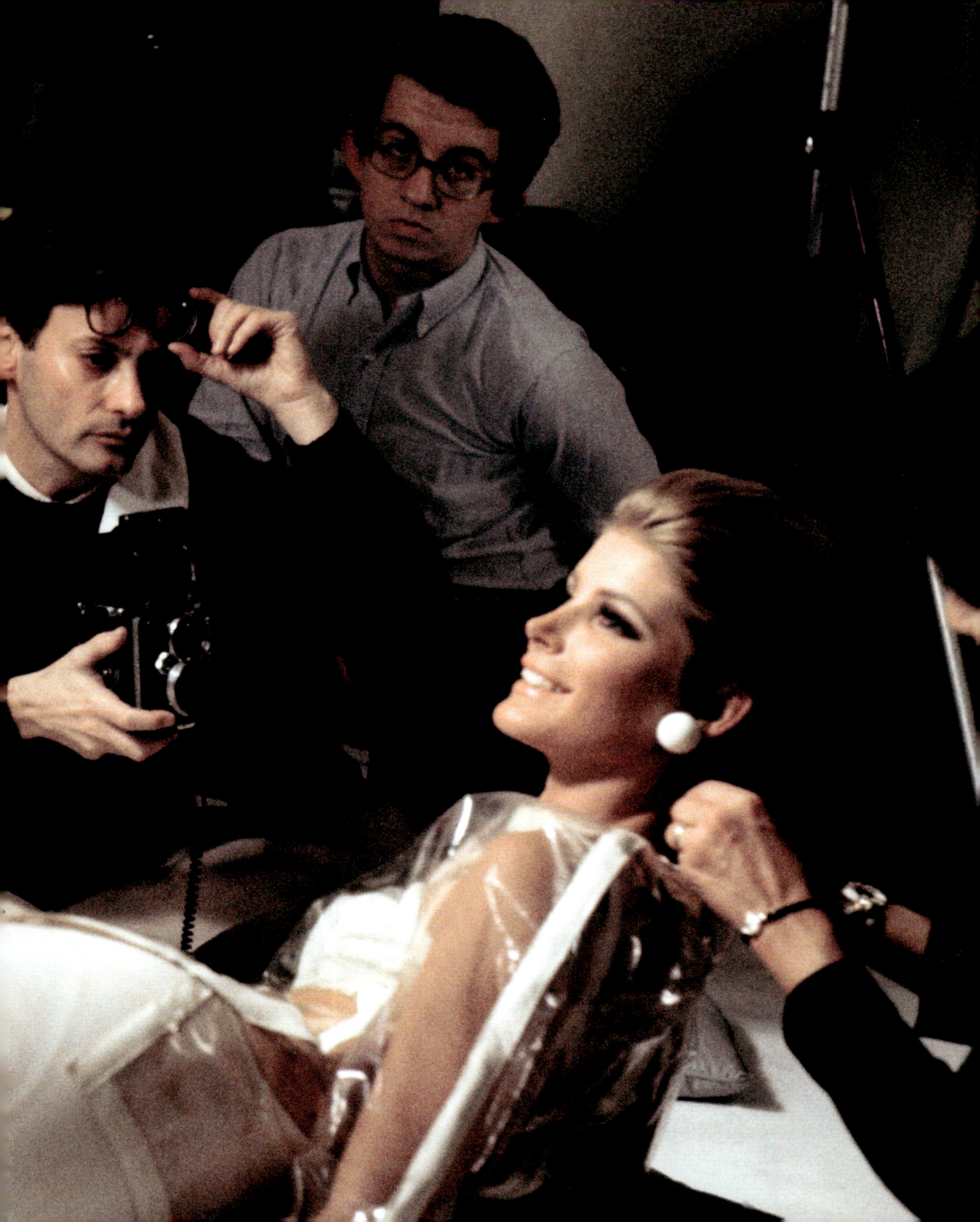

Donna Jordan

Donna Jordan is New York glam meets Hollywood elegance. Her work
as a model was and remains a brilliant study in a sort of caricature-kitsch
couture. With her bleached brows and that huge electric gap-toothed
grin, Donna has a tongue-in-chic glamour that I have always found in-
credibly inspiring and absolutely irresistible.

Marc Jacobs

Photography by Guy Bourdin

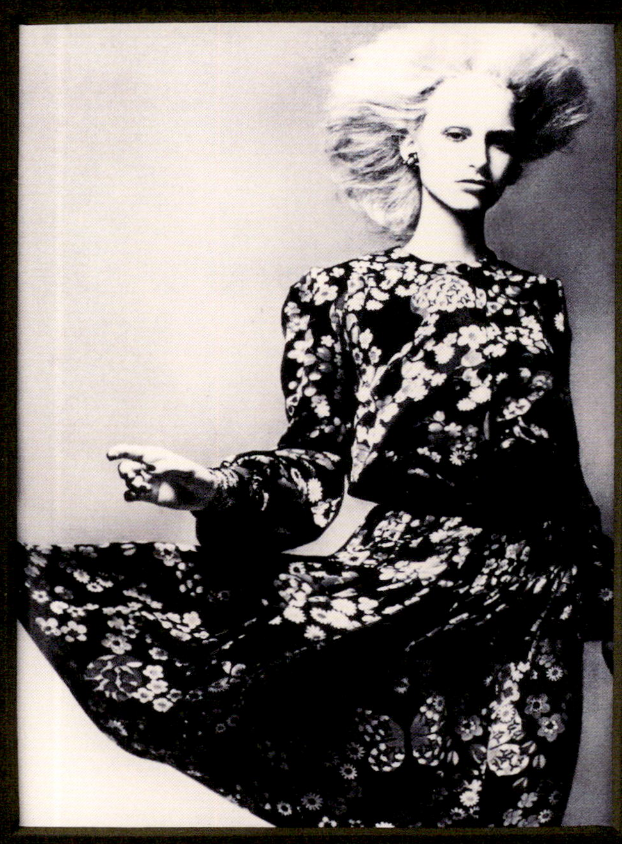

Erin O'Connor

If Erin O'Connor didn't already exist, Alexander McQueen, John Galliano, or Jean-Paul Gaultier—the three designers who used her intimidating elegance to best effect—would have had to create her in the ateliers where they made their wildest dreams come true. Tall, slender, with spectral white skin and stygian black hair, she was a Gruau drawing, an Erté sketch made flesh. But for each of those designers, her natural hauteur and balletic grace served different ends. In McQueen's asylum, she was an institutionalized aristocrat, tearing distractedly at the razor clam shells that covered her dress. At Galliano's Ballets Russes, she was a *grande dame* in Poiret. For Gaultier, she embodied the spirit of Parisian couture at its most classic, a Jacqueline de Ribes for the twenty-first century. And all the time, this apogee of sophistication was a wry, funny girl from the British Midlands, barely past her teenage years.

Modeling performs a curious alchemy on its most successful practitioners. Erin O'Connor was a perfect illustration of that transformative process. She has since accumulated the kind of experiences that deepen and enrich beauty: motherhood, social activism. And she's still modeling, although the work is no longer as heady as it was at the turn of the century. But her extraordinary look prevails: the pale skin, the dark hair, and the level, slightly hooded gaze, which could almost be drolly assessing you from some other time, far away.

Tim Blanks

Photography by Steven Meisel

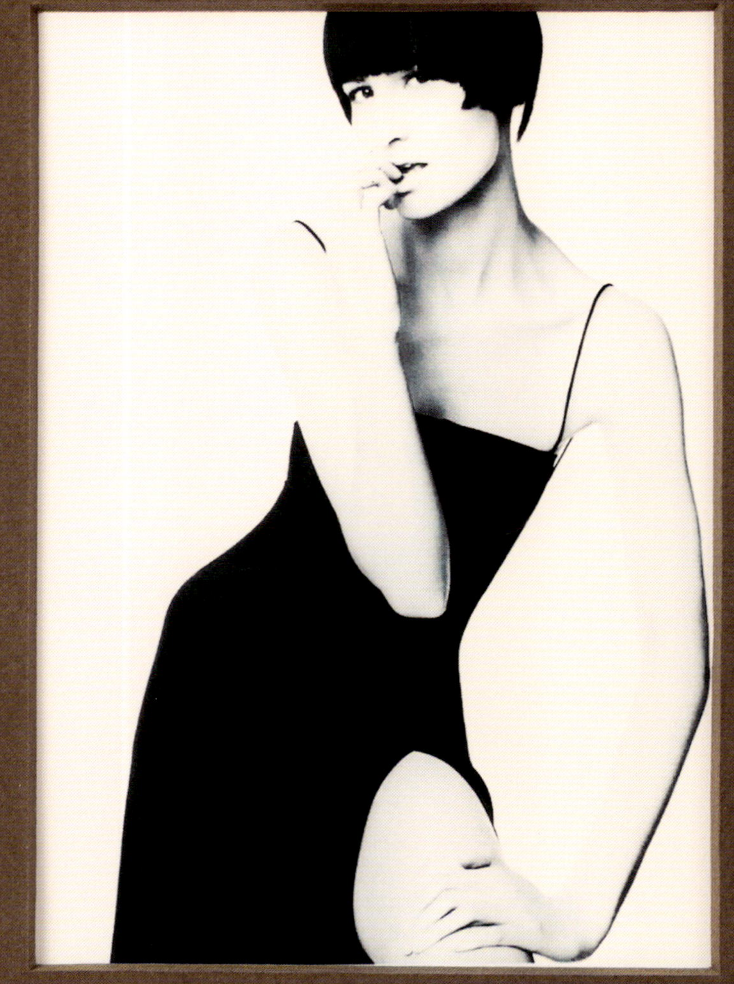

Claudia, I just let her smoke.

Juergen Teller

Photography by Juergen Teller

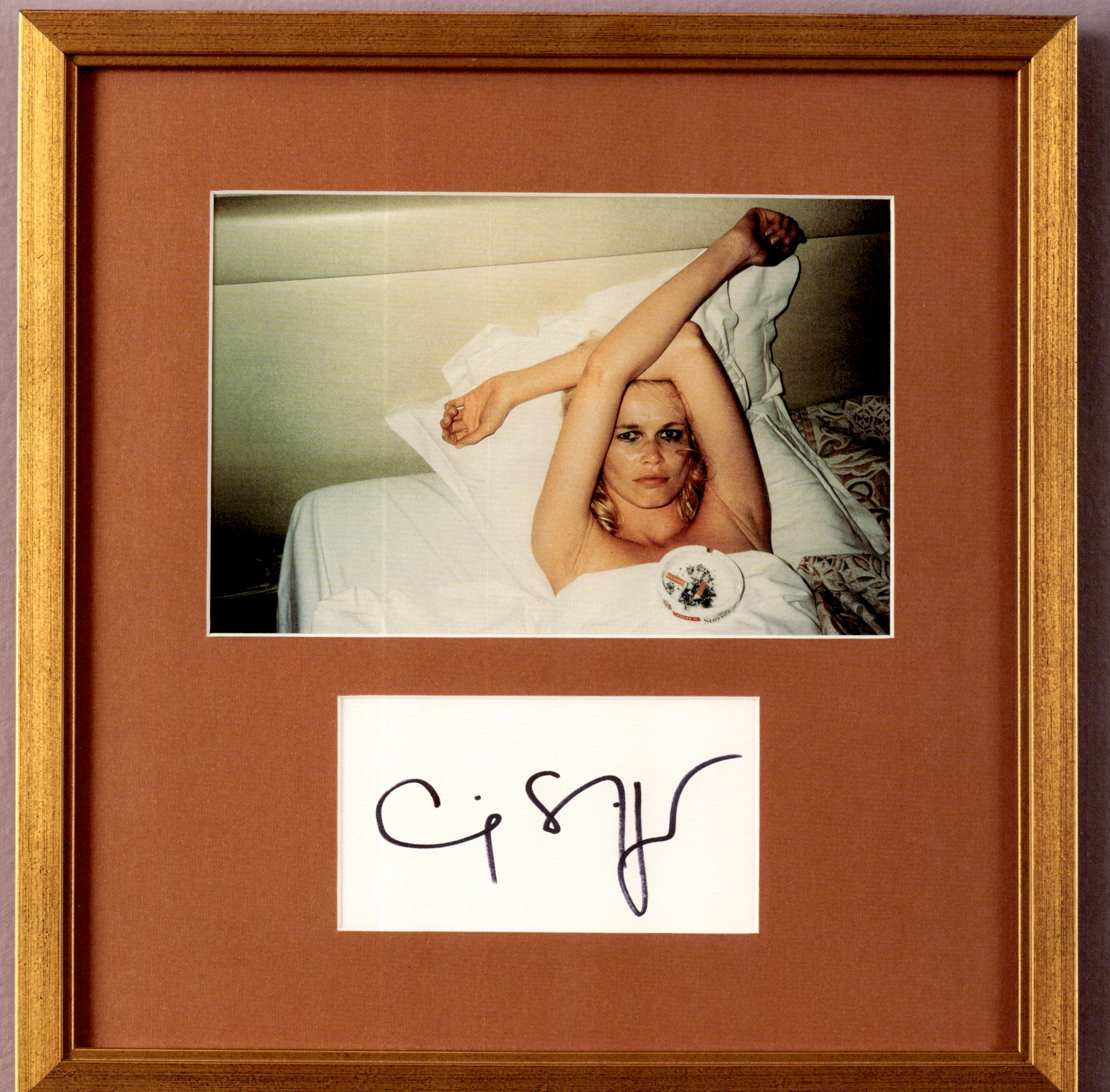

Genevieve Waite.

My friend. My angel. My love. My darling.

So many great memories. I worked with her as a fellow actor in the movie *Joanna*, where she played the pivotal role. In fact, we have a dish at Mr. Chow named after her: chicken Joanna.

The crowning moment was when I opened Mr. Chow, London, on February 14, 1968, Valentine's Day, which was also her birthday. That magical evening, I presented her with a gigantic birthday cake. Memories fade, but that moment, almost half a century ago, is imprinted on my brain.

Michael Chow

Photography by Richard Avedon

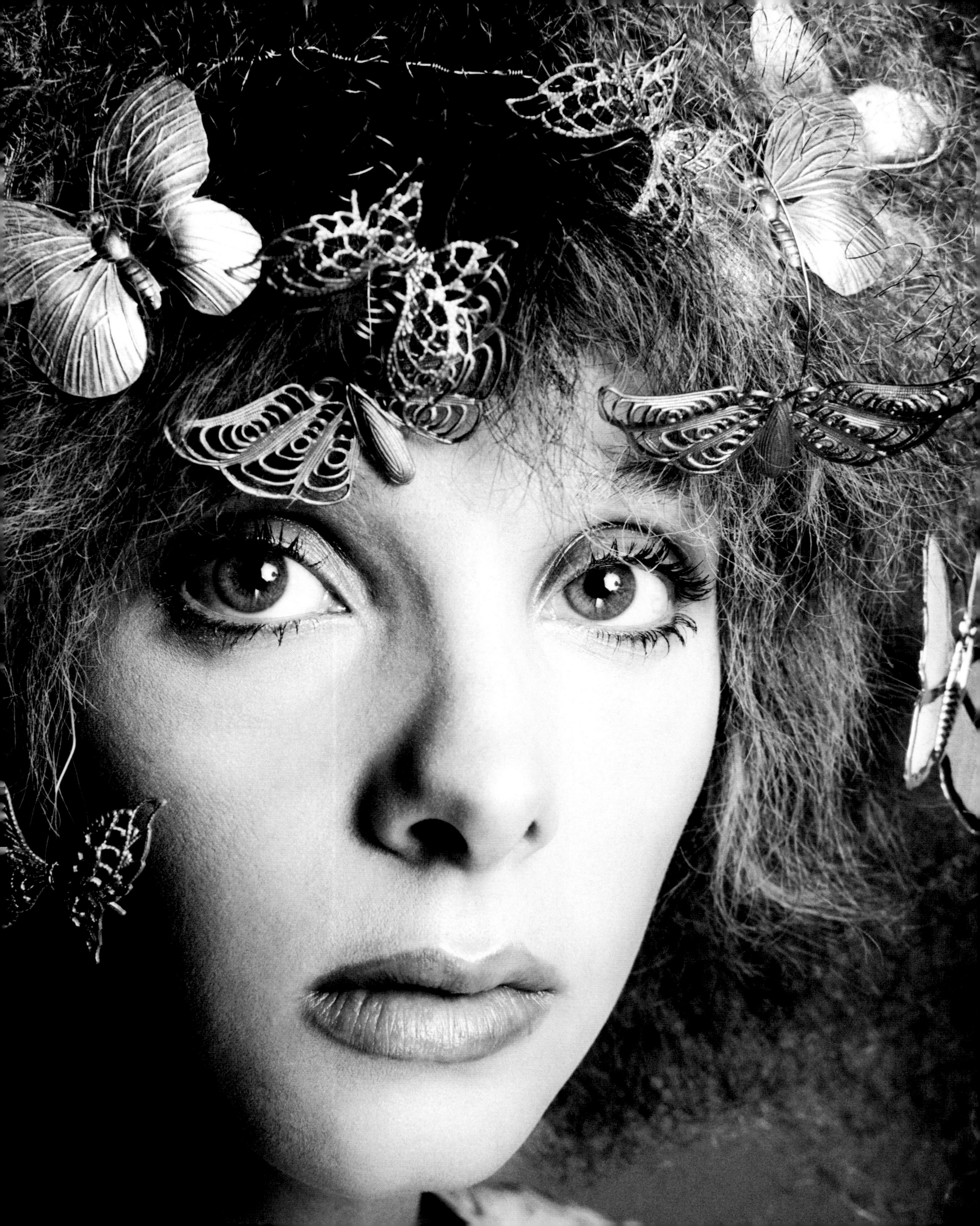

LINDA EVANGELISTA a.k.a. EVANGELOS

Best accomplice!
Best supermodel!
Best time always!
Best true friend!
Best fun!
Best fights!
Best work always!
Best "les jambes"!
Best hostess!
Best souvenirs!!!

EVANGELOS IS:
THE BEST OF THE BEST... LA CREME DE LA CREME!!!

"SALE BITCH" is the best compliment I can give. Only a few will
understand!!!!

VOILÀ!

THIS IS MON EVANGELOS THAT I LOVE... MY FAMILY!
ALWAYS ALWAYS ALWAYS!
CAPISH?

Carlyne Cerf de Dudzeele

Photography by Steven Meisel

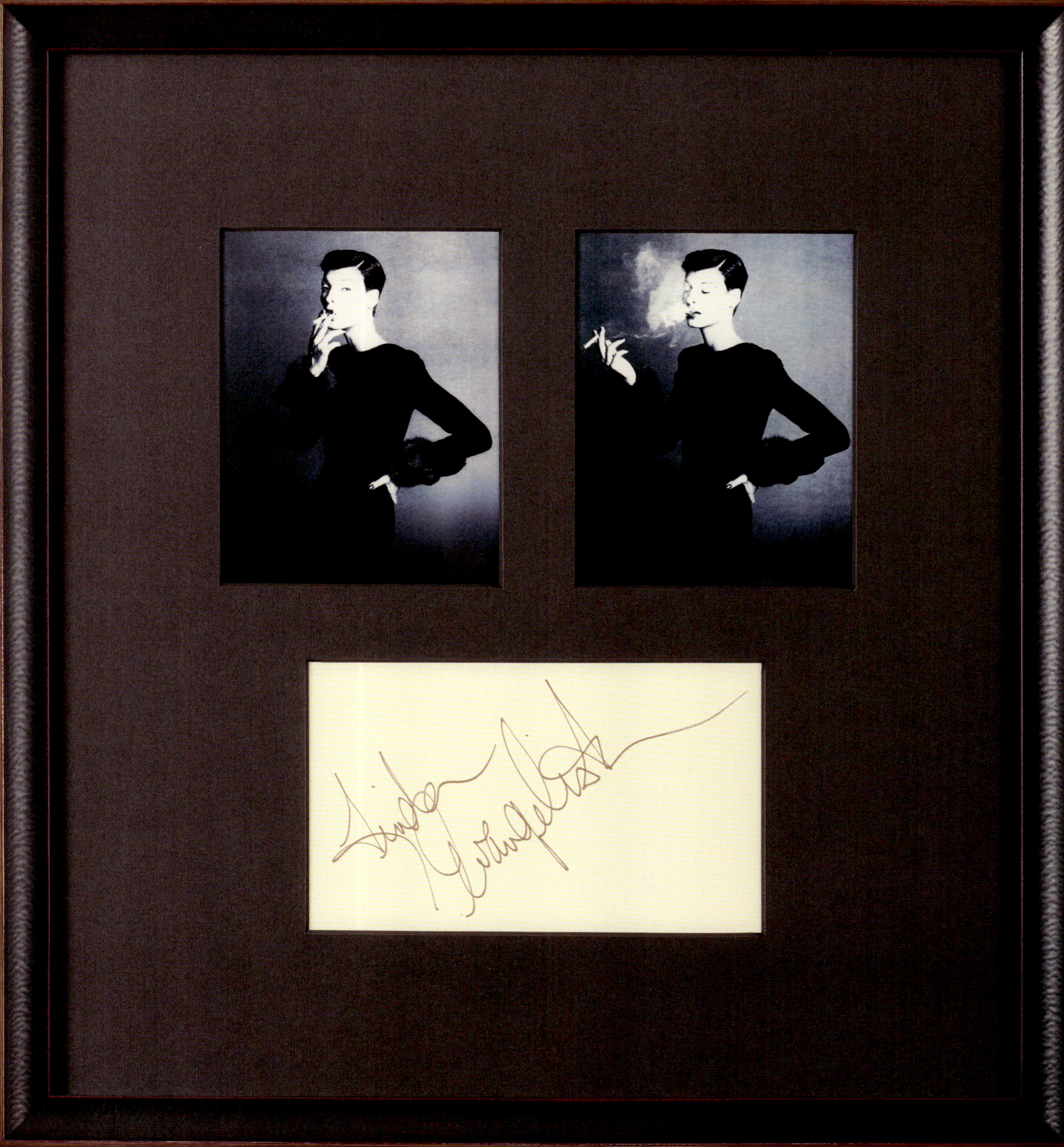

I met Ingmari in 1970. She was one of the first models I worked with, but she was already a top model and an idol to me. Her first show for Jungle Jap was in New York in 1971, and then she worked for us again in Japan.

When our Spring 1973 show came around, she had an eye condition, so I thought she wouldn't be able to walk the runway. In the end she wore a scarf over her eye, which added an undeniable touch of style to all the outfits she wore.

I will always remember the day I saw her wearing her husband's jacket. This vision inspired me to create an oversized jacket for both men and women to wear.

Ingmari has a great deal of taste and character; she is very independent and curious. Later, I began asking her advice on accessorizing my fashion shows. And then, we became the best of friends.

Kenzo Takada

Photography by Bob Richardson

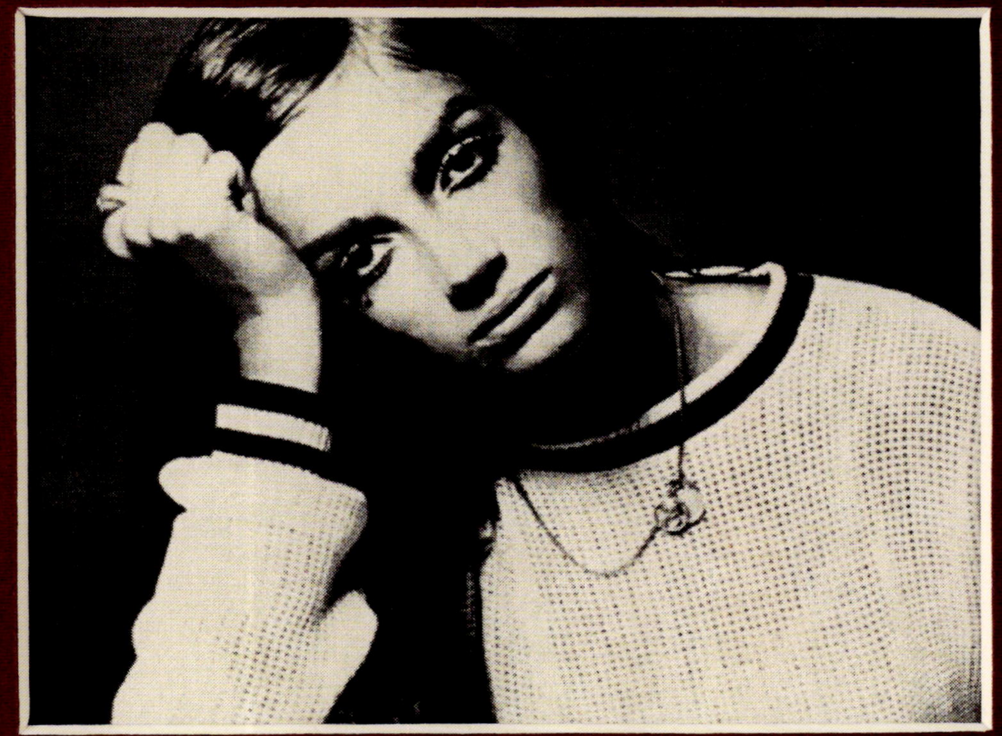

We Love Creation ♡

It was 1967. My wife discovered Naomi working in the stockroom of Bergdorf Goodman, where Halston at that time was designing only hats. Struck by her beauty and natural grace, she immediately sent Naomi to see me. I was always searching for unknown faces—not seasoned models, but ones like Naomi. Women who were not spoiled by automatic poses. Women with character first.

We didn't choose Naomi for the cover shoot of the *New York Times* fashion supplement thinking that she would be the first African-American model on a major cover. She was just the most powerful girl for the moment. My wife, who was the editor on that job, dressed her simply, in a black Halston hat and cape that accentuated her elegant features. Who wouldn't want to see that face!

But the fact that she was black did cause a stir among some of the editors. We stayed strong with our choice because we wanted to see her shine. She was nervous at first but her instinct was always to be graceful, and that came out in her photographs.

Gosta Peterson

Photography by Gosta Peterson

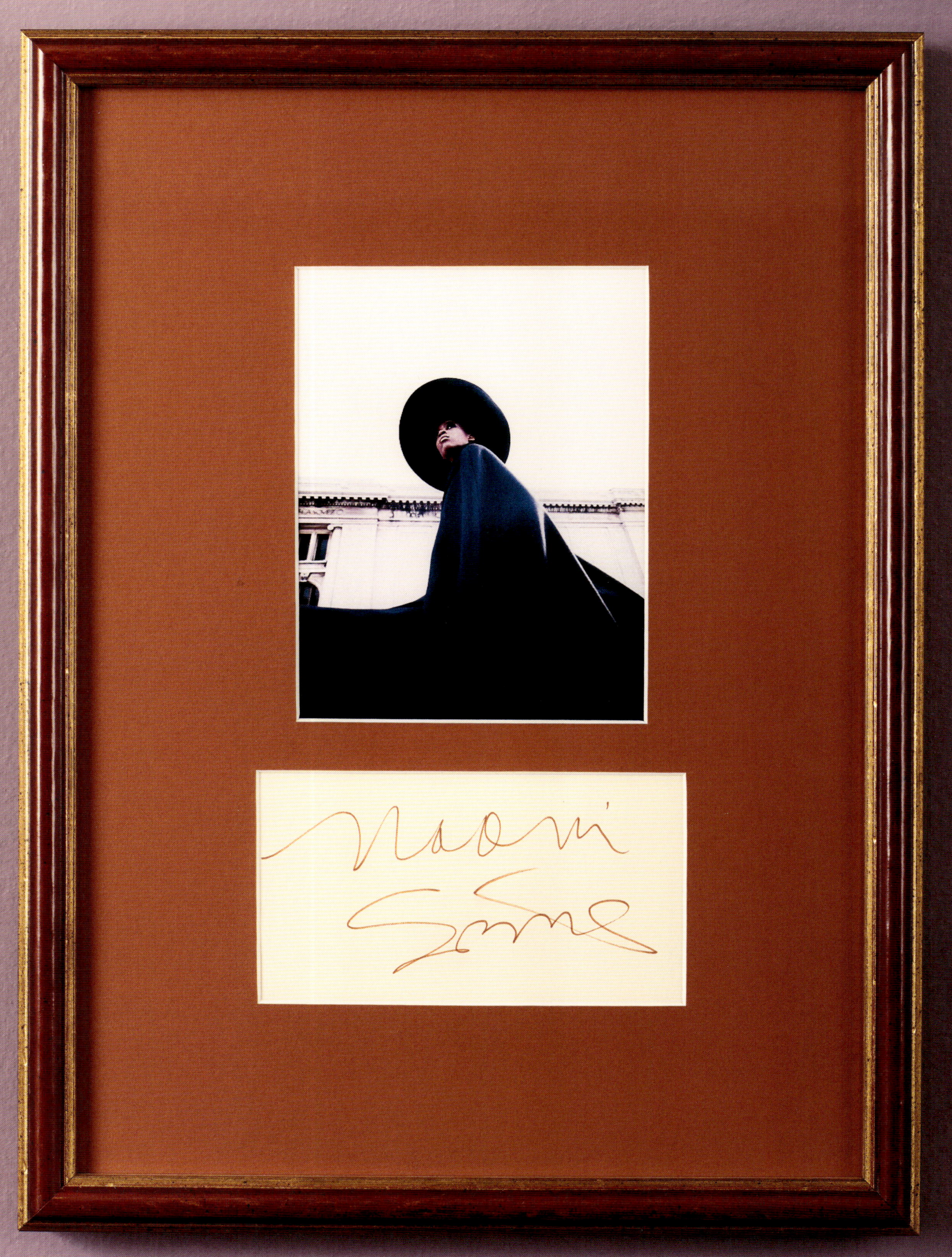
Naomi
Some

Jane Holzer

In the spring of 1963, Nicky Haslam, a plugged-in young Englishman then working in the art department of *Vogue*, took Andy Warhol to a dinner at Jane Holzer's Park Avenue apartment. Jane was a twenty-two-year-old heiress from Palm Beach who had recently married New York real estate heir Lenny Holzer. As Warhol would later write in his memoir *POPism: The Warhol '6os*, "David Bailey was there and he'd brought the lead singer in a rock-and-roll group called the Rolling Stones that was then playing the northern cities of England."

A few months later, Andy ran into Jane on Madison Avenue: "She was such a gorgeous girl—great skin and hair. And so much enthusiasm—she wanted to do everything." He asked her if she would be in one of the underground movies he was making almost daily at his studio, known as the Factory. "Sure! Anything beats being a Park Avenue housewife," she famously replied. "I wanted to have fun," she later explained. "I wanted to be a star!"

And so she was: an American Bardot in Courrèges, Cardin, and Paco Rabanne couture, "a Holly Golightly for the Mod era, but with her own money," as the *Palm Beach Post* put it. Warhol christened her Baby Jane Holzer, his first superstar, in a line that would come to include Edie Sedgwick, Viva, Nico, Ultra Violet, International Velvet, Brigid Polk, Jackie Curtis, Holly Woodlawn, and Candy Darling. In quick succession he featured her in *Soap Opera*, *Couch*, *Camp*, and *The 13 Most Beautiful Women in the World*. "Jane Holzer is the most contemporary girl I know," declared *Vogue*'s editor-in-chief Diana Vreeland, who ran big fashion spreads of Jane photographed by Irving Penn and David Bailey. Bailey also shot her for the cover of supermarket scion Huntington Hartford's new magazine *Show*, with sunglasses from the 1964 New York World's Fair hiding her eyes and an American flag clenched between her teeth. No wonder Tom Wolfe anointed her "Girl of the Year" in a *New York* magazine profile that was subsequently published as a chapter in *The Kandy-Kolored Tangerine-Flake Streamline Baby*, the book that secured both his literary reputation and her status as a pop culture legend.

Jane was never one to stand still when moving fast was so much more exciting. She went on to become a film producer, the proprietor of a Palm Beach ice cream parlor, a real estate developer, and a leading collector of contemporary art. Starting with the Warhol "Flowers" paintings she bought for a few hundred dollars each soon after she met him, she has gone on to fill her houses in Manhattan, Southampton, and Palm Beach with works by such new-generation stars as Christopher Wool, Rudolf Stingel, and the Bruce High Quality Foundation.

In 2014, West Palm Beach celebrated its most famous daughter with an exhibition at the Norton Museum of Art titled "To Jane, Love Andy," featuring everything from her art collection to her white patent leather go-go boots. In recognition of her longstanding patronage of the arts, the New York Academy of Art, which Warhol helped found in 1980, honored her at their annual gala in 2016.

The Girl of the Year had become the hippest *grande dame* of her generation.

Bob Colacello

Photography by Irving Penn

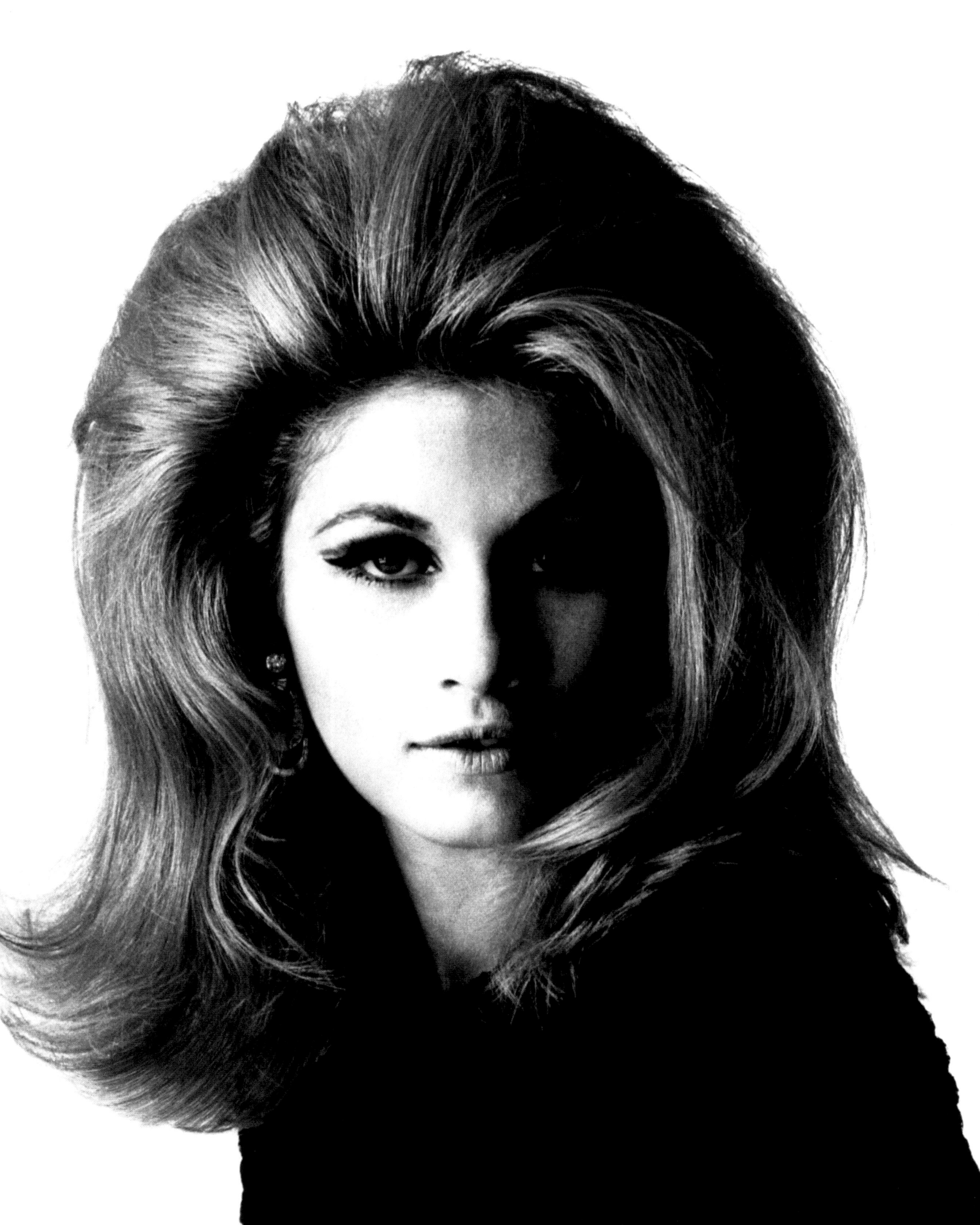

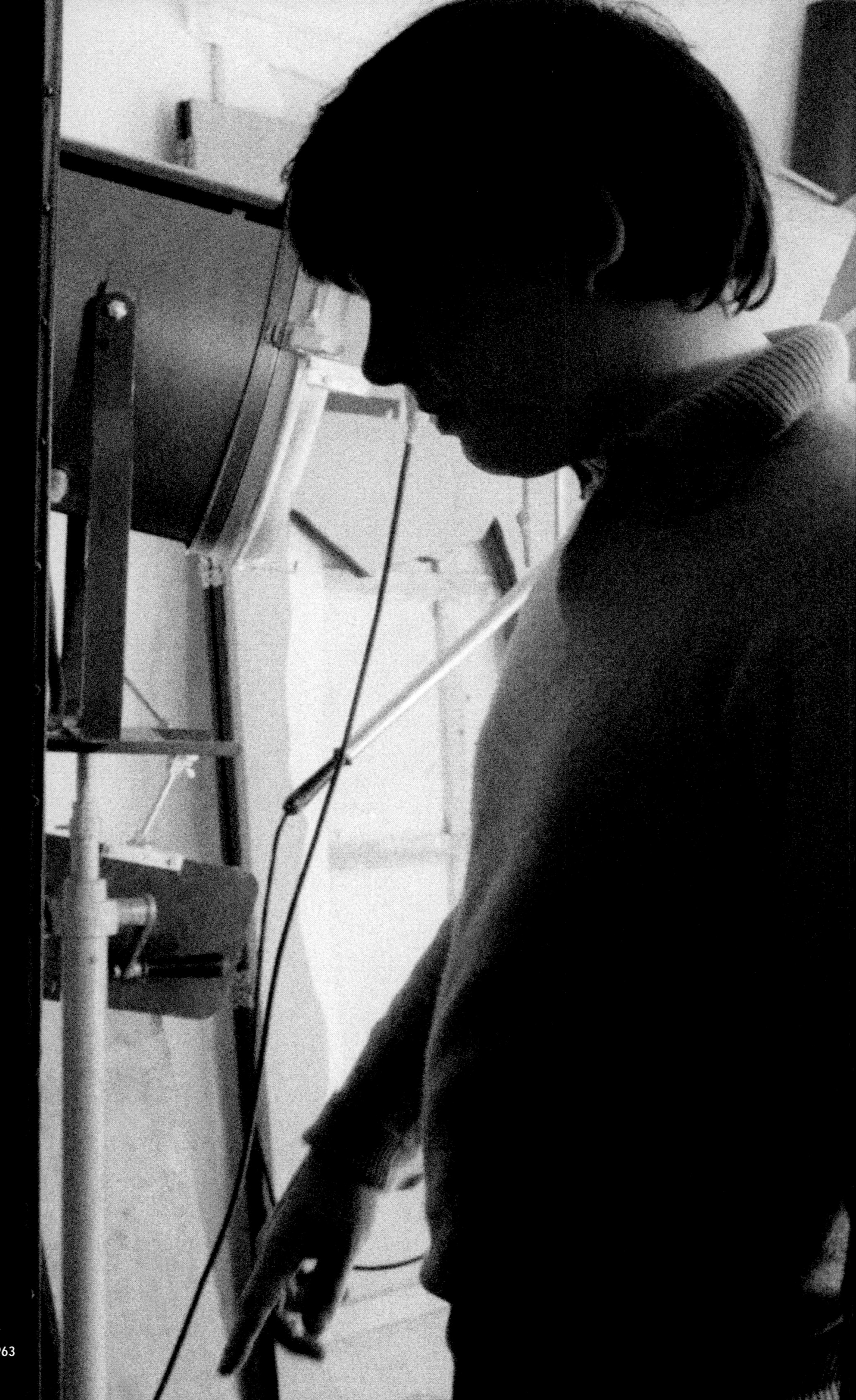

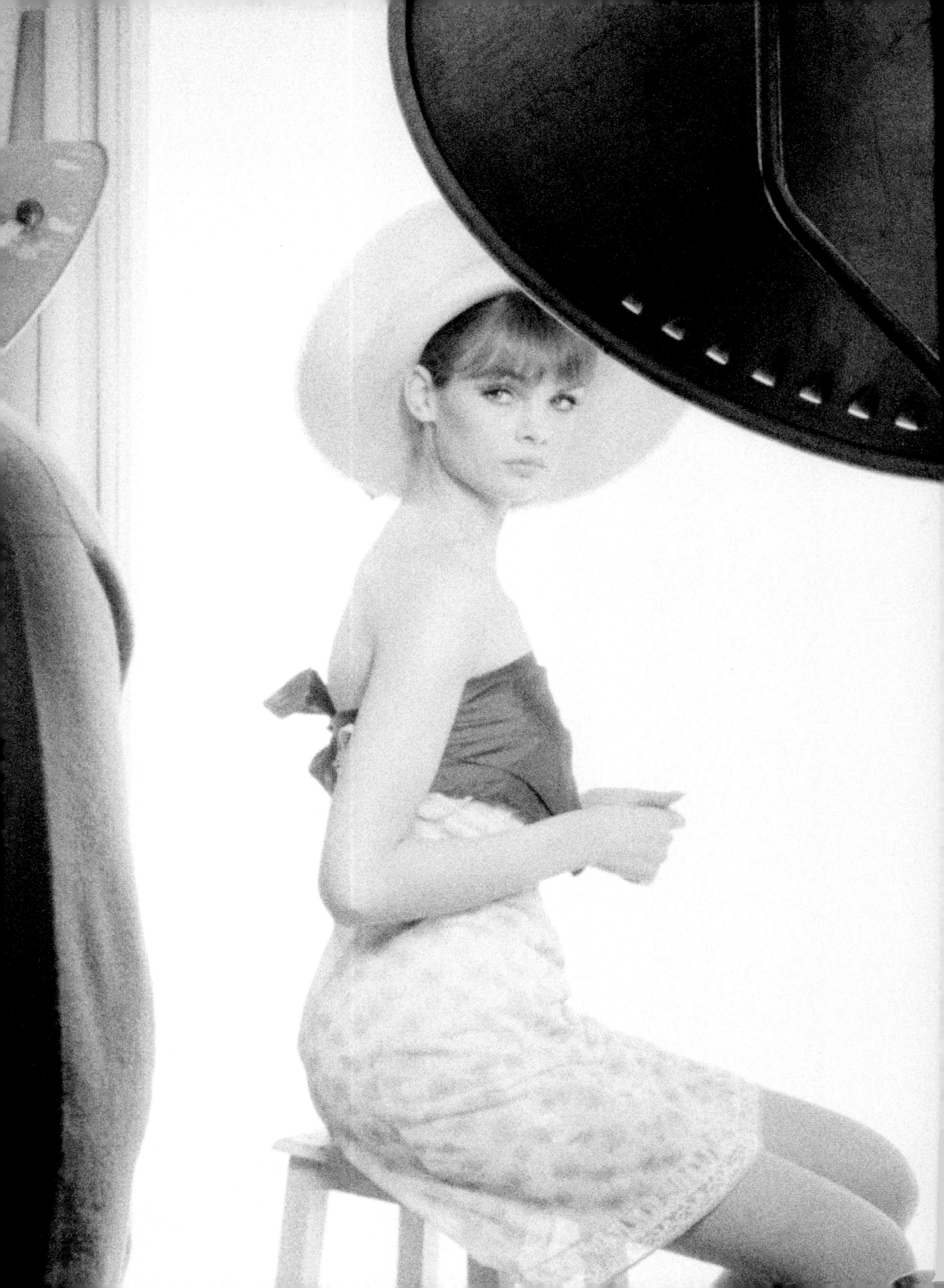

Anita Pallenberg

Anita Pallenberg: just her name is an enigma.

Everybody knows that name. And they think they know who she is. You can see snatches of uninformed gossip and half-understood truth flash across their faces when they hear it: Black magic queen. Drug addict. The gorgeous woman in *Barbarella*. Keith Richards's first wife. The best-dressed woman in rock 'n roll; the one that everybody copies still—even Kate Moss says it! She's a public figure, after all; she's part of history. The faces take on that look of desperation and readymade skepticism.

But in fact, they don't know a thing about her.

We met at a party in London thirteen years ago through an ex-boyfriend of mine. We hit it off—maybe because I had no interest in being her friend. (I knew she was someone, but I didn't know who she was.) She grabbed me and said, "I like how you don't smile at anyone ever," so of course that made me smile at her and that was that. She really doesn't want any new friends. Or rather, the new friends she has are not the friends you'd expect, such as the ladies with whom she gardens in a Chelsea allotment.

Anita might be the ne plus ultra rock 'n roll chick, yet she comes from an exceedingly refined, educated background. Her grandfather was the late Romantic, Decadent German painter Arnold Böcklin; his painting *Isle of the Dead* hangs in the Metropolitan Museum of Art. She got a degree from St. Martin's School of Art in her fifties and started painting in her sixties, and some of her paintings are damn great. She's a savant.

Anita is a devoted grandmother now and lives mostly in Jamaica. (She was in jail in Ocho Rios in 1978; that might give you a sense of another side of Anita Pallenberg.) You'll never catch Anita reminiscing about the past. That's not her thing. She's a figure out of history who lives entirely in the present—and I have had the privilege of being part of that present. She is an icon.

Stella Schnabel

Photography by Unknown

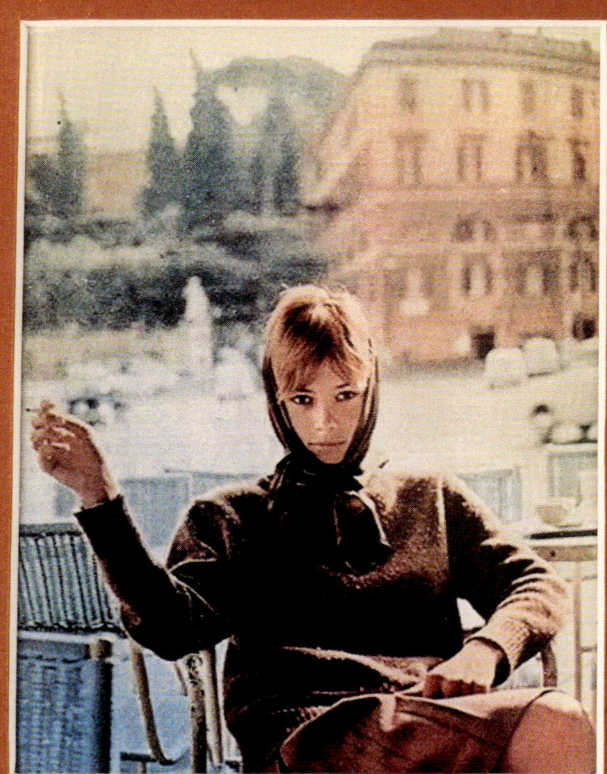

Farida Khelfa

Farida is my friend, but she also is a character out of a novel, full of contradictions: fierce and warm, impulsive and tender, perfectly put together down to the tips of her fingers yet simple as hello. She is like a queen, famous yet mysterious; she is like a flower growing up through the concrete of the city. Her life story makes you want to live large, and to believe in fairy tales.

As a top model, an actress, a director, and a producer, she has built her life with talent yet without pretension, simply with studious application and hard work. She never forgets where she came from; she has transformed her roots into blossoms. Besides her intelligence, her undeniable charm, and her absolute elegance on all occasions (and by that I mean also an elegance of the soul), what I like most about Farida is her enormous generosity. Farida is profoundly kind to all who cross her path, to all who might need her love or support. Farida is my friend, and I am lucky.

Carla Bruni

Photography by Jean Paul Goude

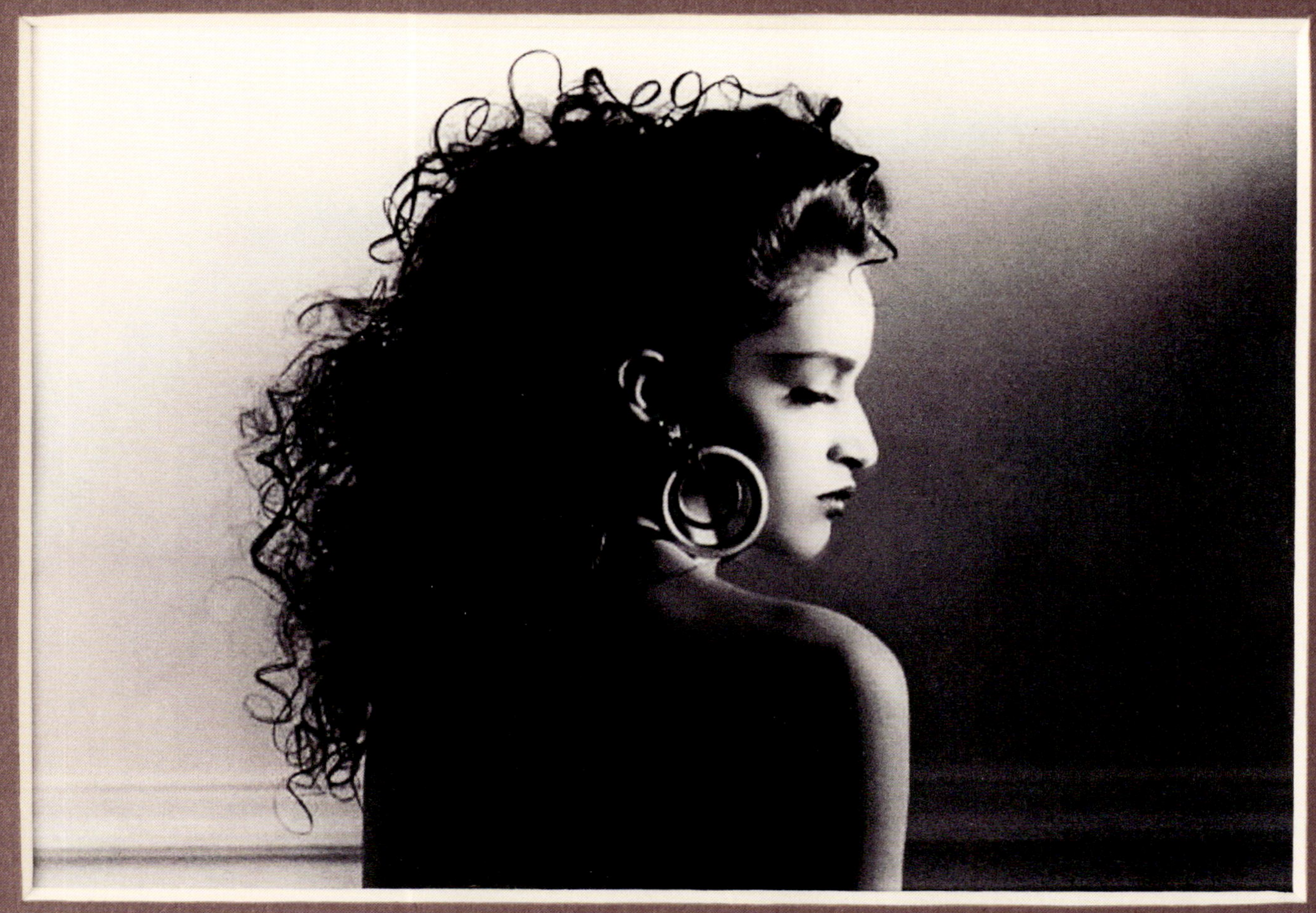

Farida.

Star quality and the energy of a supernova—Pat Cleveland was born with "it."

I first caught her light and presence at a party at Henri Bendel in 2001—a moment that felt as if it was frozen in time, like something out of *West Side Story*. I was mesmerized; I could see and feel her marvelousness from across the room. We became friends. At the time, I didn't know much about Pat or her lasting contribution to fashion.

In 1966, when she was sixteen, Pat was scouted by *Vogue*'s Carrie Donovan on a subway platform, on her way to the High School of the Performing Arts. Carrie brought her to the original star-maker and ultimate arbiter of fashion, the one and only Diana Vreeland. Vreeland had Pat photographed in clothes she'd made herself.

Pat joined the Ebony Fashion Fair tour, but soon decided to leave the United States, with its racial prejudice and discrimination. In Europe, she found fame and success, as Josephine Baker had done forty years earlier. Encouraged by the illustrator Antonio Lopez, Pat settled in Paris, where she became the flavor of the moment and inspired many great creators: Halston, Lagerfeld, Mugler, Moschino (to name just a few). She returned to the U.S. only after a girl of color had appeared on the cover of *Vogue*.

Wherever she was, Pat Cleveland was the star of the runway. She is the ultimate interpreter of the garments she shows: fully committed, expressive, and fearless as she brings the clothes to life. Pat was a pioneer of runway as theater, in collaboration with extraordinary designers. Decades later, she continues to weave her magic on the runway.

Pat is a person of breathtaking honesty and deep feeling; she herself is poetry, and the poems she writes are beautiful and sensitive. Most of all, she is full of joy. I remain her fan and her friend. And I love to watch her walk.

Zac Posen

Photography by Horst

Joy
2010 N.Y.C. USA
Pat Cleveland
Love you
guys
Big Hug XXX
from love
me

Anjelica Huston

Before the flash and the shutter freeze her in sepia-tinted color, it all be-gins with a name: Anjelica. Which, thanks to the association of ideas and images, leads us back to a cult 1960s French film: *Angélique, Marquise of Angels*. A noble title, but as illusory as an apparition that fell to earth or the sudden appearance of a reflection in a mirror, perhaps the flicker of the black lace fan that crowns her head and encircles it with a halo.

The gaze returns incessantly to that fan, descends along the gloved arms with their sensual grace, which set the tone for all that will happen, all that will pass. This, despite her pose verging on the improbable: she hov-ers as if somehow emerging from the bust of the black virgin, creating a Cubist-like split, an homage to Picasso. And, perhaps because of the balance created by the ovals of the two faces, a word springs to mind: "muse." Both glamorous inspiration and *femme fatale*. High priestess for all eternity, she poses under the spotlights, among the thrown shadows, while her bugle-beaded embroidered dress, glittering with gold, illumi-nates her as the composition's main character.

Then there is her other name, the one she inherited from her legendary father, whose protective shadow hangs over this image. John Huston: world-famous wandering filmmaker, Hollywood royalty and cinematic rebel. Yet here his spectral presence conjures up not a legendary scene from *The Asphalt Jungle* or *The Misfits*, but rather Anjelica in *Prizzi's Honor*, a performance that earned her a best supporting actress Oscar. Particularly the ball scene: her arms similarly sheathed in skin-tight black gloves, her shoulders barely covered by a shocking pink stole, her presence so enigmatic, so moving.

Before the anecdotal became the historical, though, it was 1973 when Da-vid Bailey shot this image for British *Vogue* at Karl Lagerfeld's Left Bank apartment on rue Saint-Sulpice, using the existing decor as a sensual yet detached frame, as if he were sketching at the heart of a bigger picture. The end result illustrates something almost quintessential about its sub-ject's life: the moment when Anjelica began her shift, her transition, her metamorphosis even, from the classic poses of the model to the perfor-mances of the actress she would become.

Pamela Golbin

Photography by David Bailey

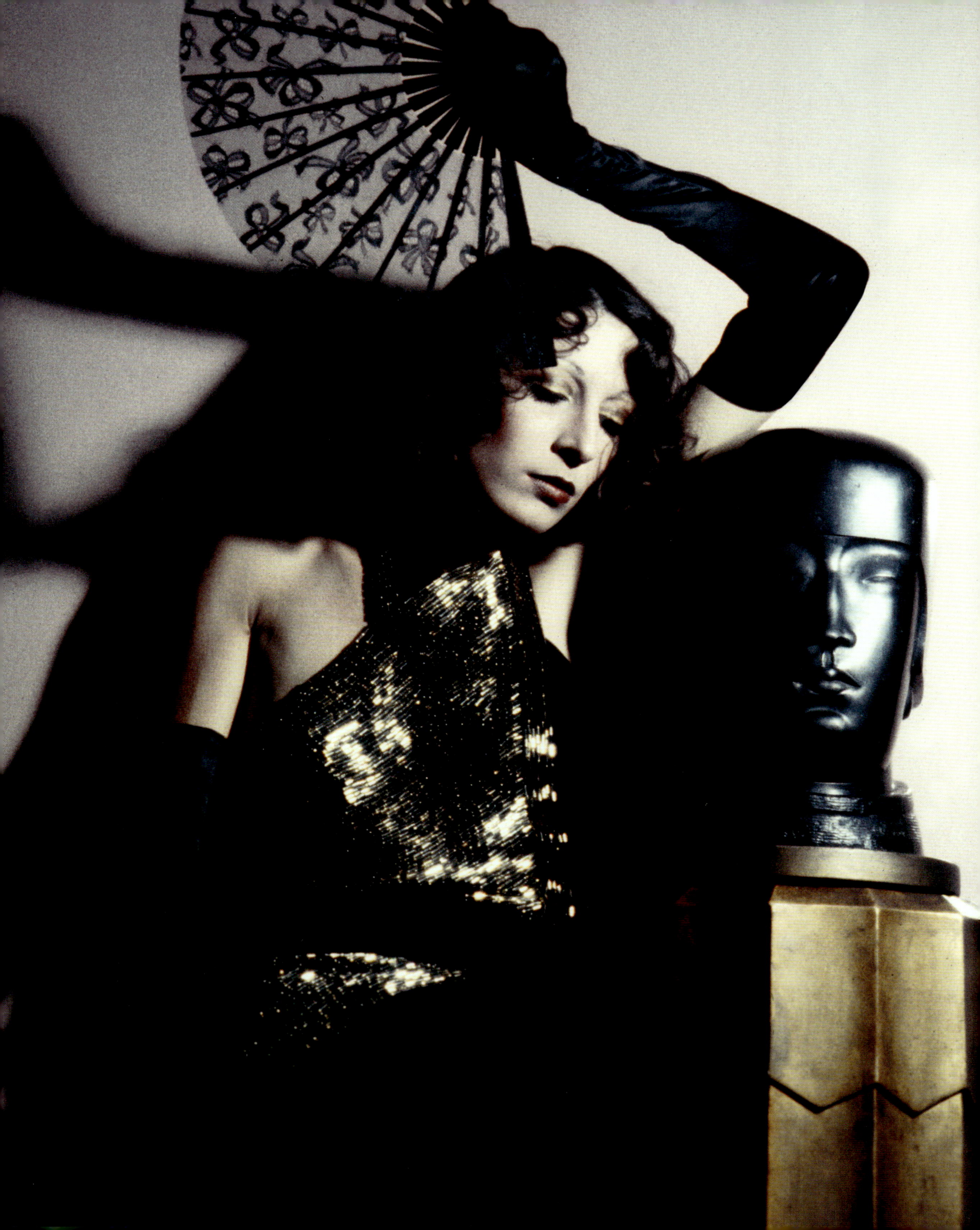

Ayumi Tanabe

hysteric glamour muse
90s lost decade yamato nadeshiko
tokyo's indie overthrow

Tiffany Godoy

Photography by Steven Meisel

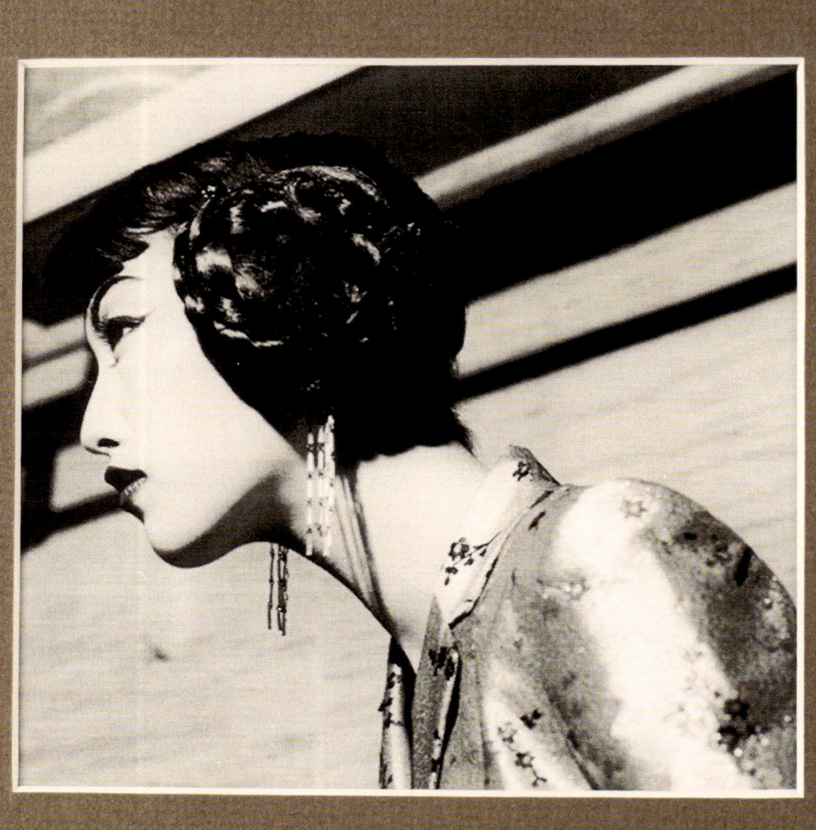

Beverly Johnson

I first laid eyes on Beverly when she came into the atelier Narcissa on East 58th Street, New York, where I was working as a fit model and assistant to the designer, Eric Lund. Eric had asked to meet her. It was, basically, a "go-see."

Beverly was young and still in college. I saw her for only a brief moment: a pretty brown girl rushing past me on her way out, heading back to Boston for class. She didn't seem particularly special to me, then. There were many good-looking girls of color around, and they were becoming more visible.

In the early 1970s, after the civil rights era, the chant "Black is Beautiful" was ringing out. But still, the crossover of models of color into the mainstream was rare. Models of color were not considered for jobs where a white model would normally be used. Even today, television and feature films are more likely to use a black woman than the fashion industry, which is still fixated on reflecting its primary consumer.

In the 1970s, this was less of an issue than it is today. Black people felt that we were part of a more important reality, and that "the revolution would not be televised." No one cared about being in some white man's anything. Crossing over was selling out. The movement was about who we were as people of color; we were reflecting ourselves, our identity, and our style: fists in the air, Afro hairstyles, organizations such as the Black Panthers, the Southern Christian Leadership Conference, the Student Nonviolent Coordinating Committee, Core, and the NAACP standing up against an oppressive system. It was about protecting our rights and being taken seriously by white mainstream society.

"Black is Beautiful!" Young white advertising executives heard that chant too. They were looking for something new, and black was what was happening. It was a good time to be a girl of color in the modeling world.

I have always believed that energy creates energy. When I realized that the girl who rushed passed me that day was the first black girl on the cover of American *Vogue*, it was a thrill. I was part of her moment, and she was part of mine. It didn't matter that she wasn't rocking a 'Fro. Though, like many black women, I didn't identify with her girl-next-door image, I saw a beautiful brown girl on the cover of a national white fashion magazine. That had never happened before. And the bonus was that white women and girls were saying that they wished they looked like her. Beverly's beauty transcended race.

So it was that a black college girl with non-defiant looks began our journey into the mainstream. History was made in a realm that most militants ignored or despised. Black college men who were speaking out against the system were being branded as troublemakers, and some were locked up. I considered myself a militant, and some of those men were my friends. But I was lucky that, being in the fashion industry, I could recognize what was happening. The cover of American *Vogue* didn't seem like a battleground in the struggle, but we won it: a non-white face was chosen where a white face had always been before.

Bethann Hardison

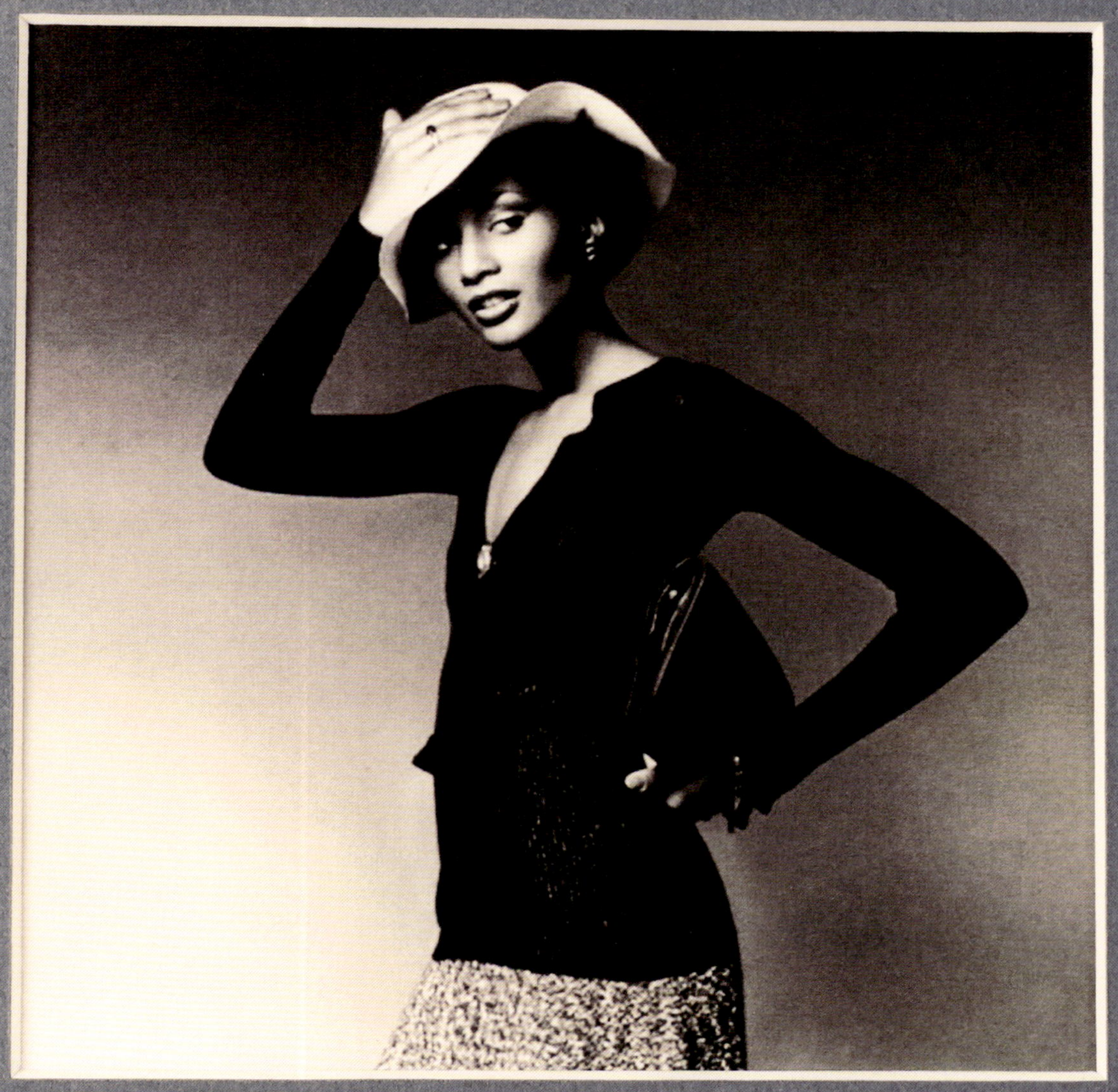

When you look at the iconic images of Penelope Tree you are transported into another world, exotic and unfamiliar. Inevitably, you are captivated by those eyes. Her gaze suggests intelligence and curiosity, her physique elegance and nobility. If I didn't know her I would wonder where she came from, and how someone so individual became celebrated as a model—a profession in which many of the alluring participants often seem interchangeable.

James Joyce, writing of the moon, speaks of the "tranquil inscrutability of her visage." That phrase captures exactly the mysterious enchantment of Penelope Tree.

Peter Eyre

Photography by Cecil Beaton

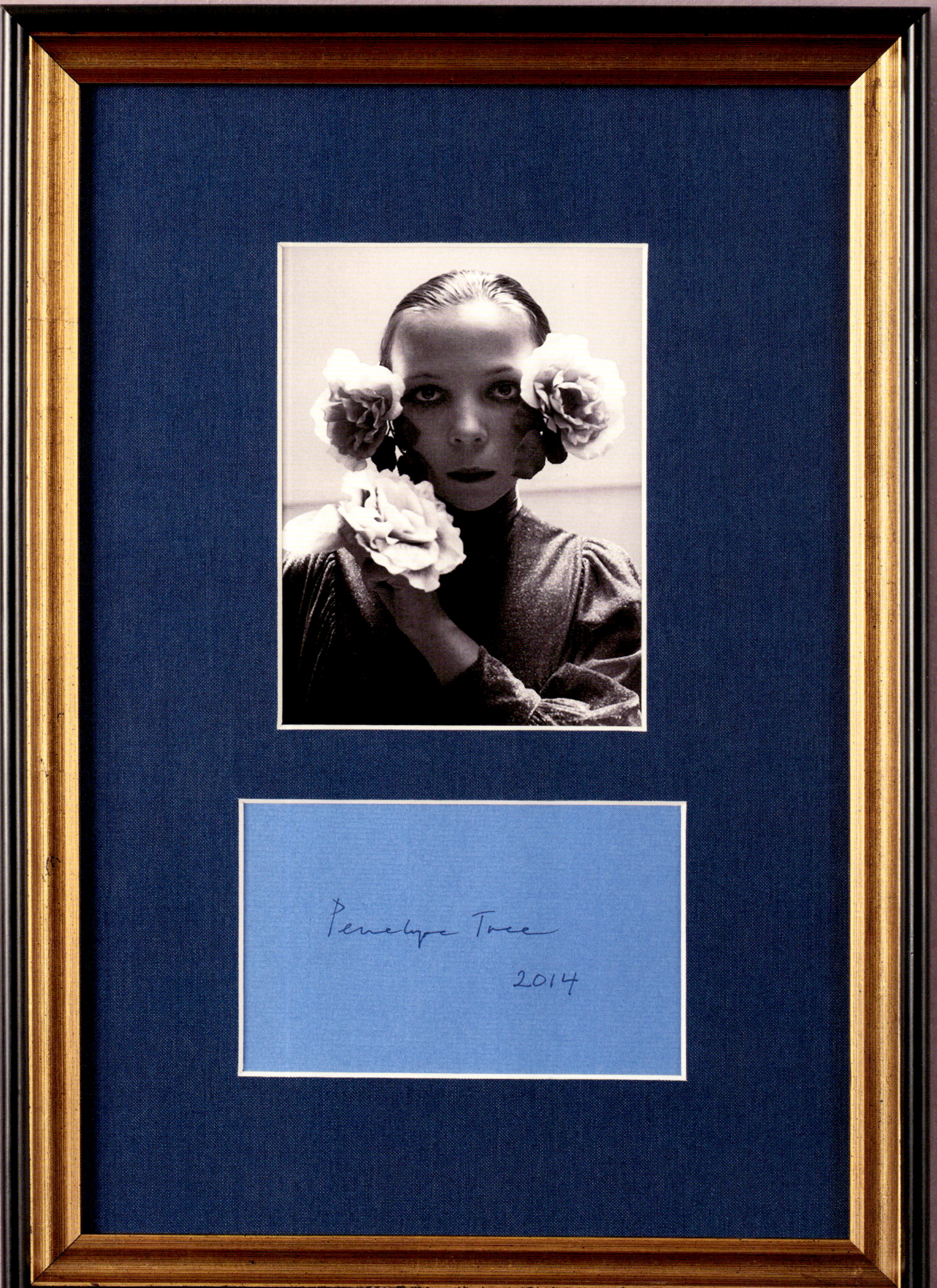

Penelope Tree
2014

Many things can be said about Isabella Rossellini: the beautiful face for
Lancôme, the top model, the actress, the animal lover...

I remember when I went to interview her some years ago, in her duplex
apartment in New York's SoHo. "The most difficult thing in my life is or-
ganizing my schedule and allocating my time," she told me. "I inherited
a taste for order and cleanliness from my mother, Ingrid Bergman, and
my Swedish family." Even though Isabella speaks with the kindness and
fluency of someone who is used to being interviewed, I sensed that at
heart she is extremely shy. When, at the end of our interview, she gra-
ciously escorted me to the door, she worried that I wouldn't be able to
find a cab, as it was rush hour. Her parting remark was, "I'll always be the
Italian mamma," to which she added, "I worry about everything."

Alain Elkann

Photography by Steven Meisel

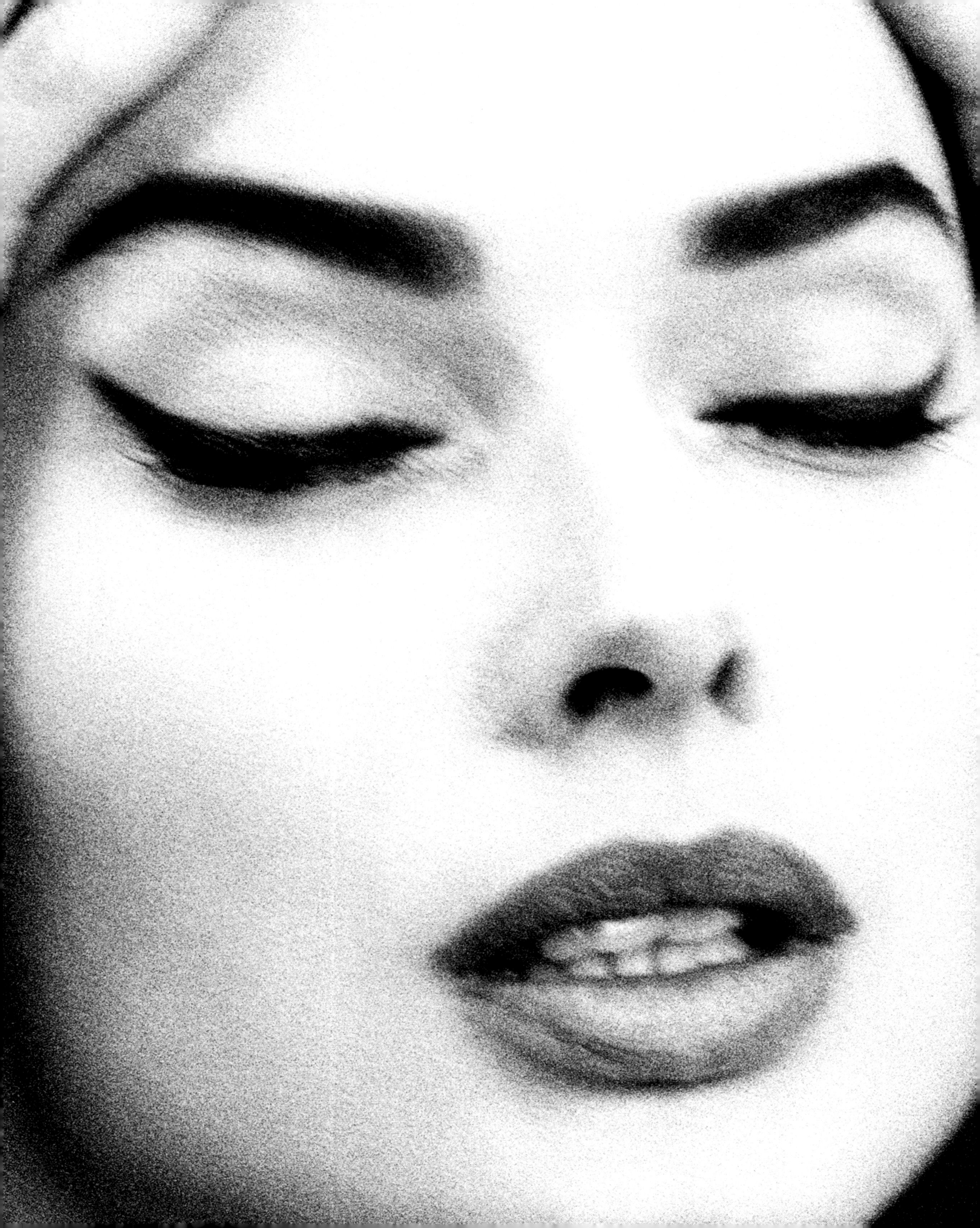

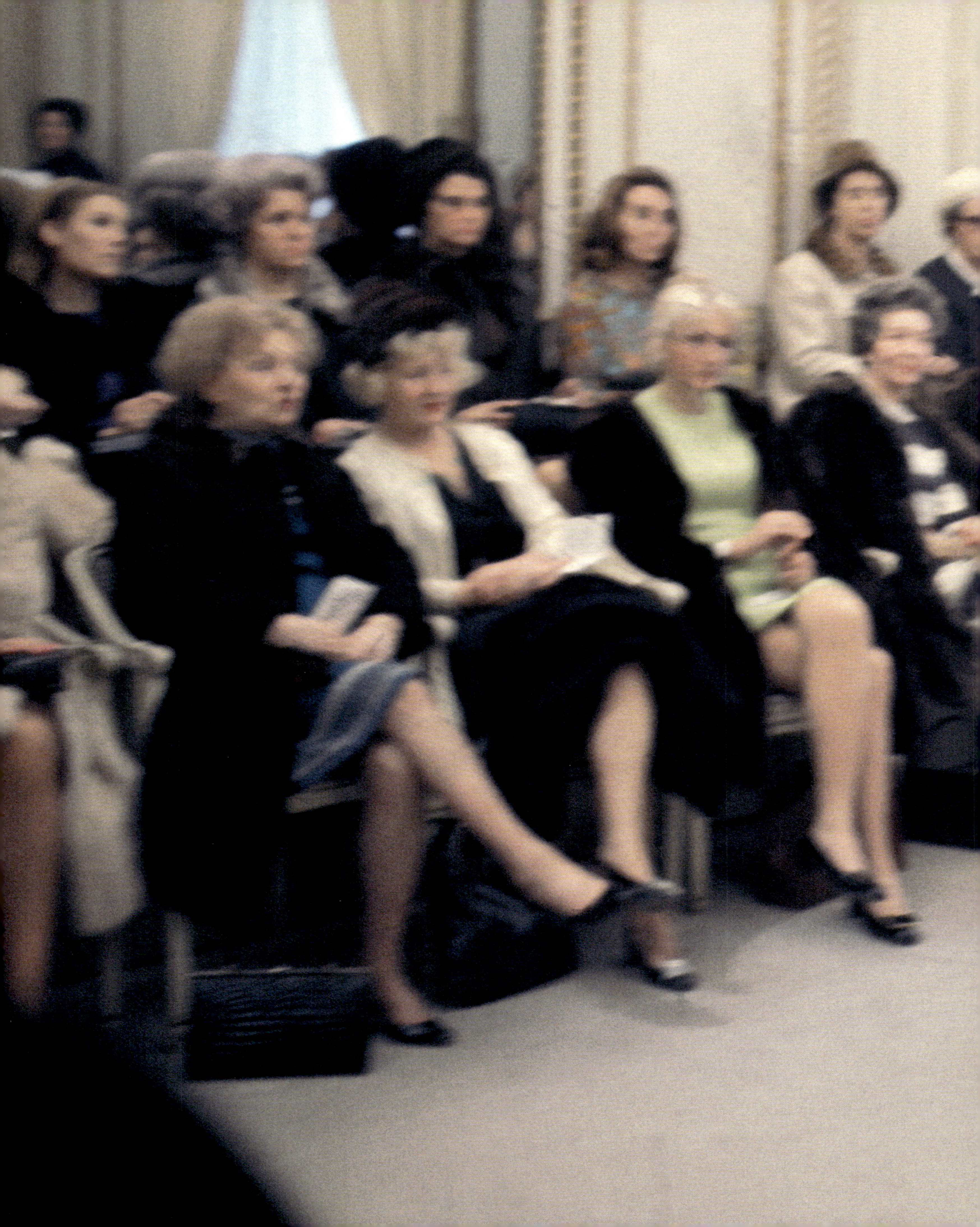

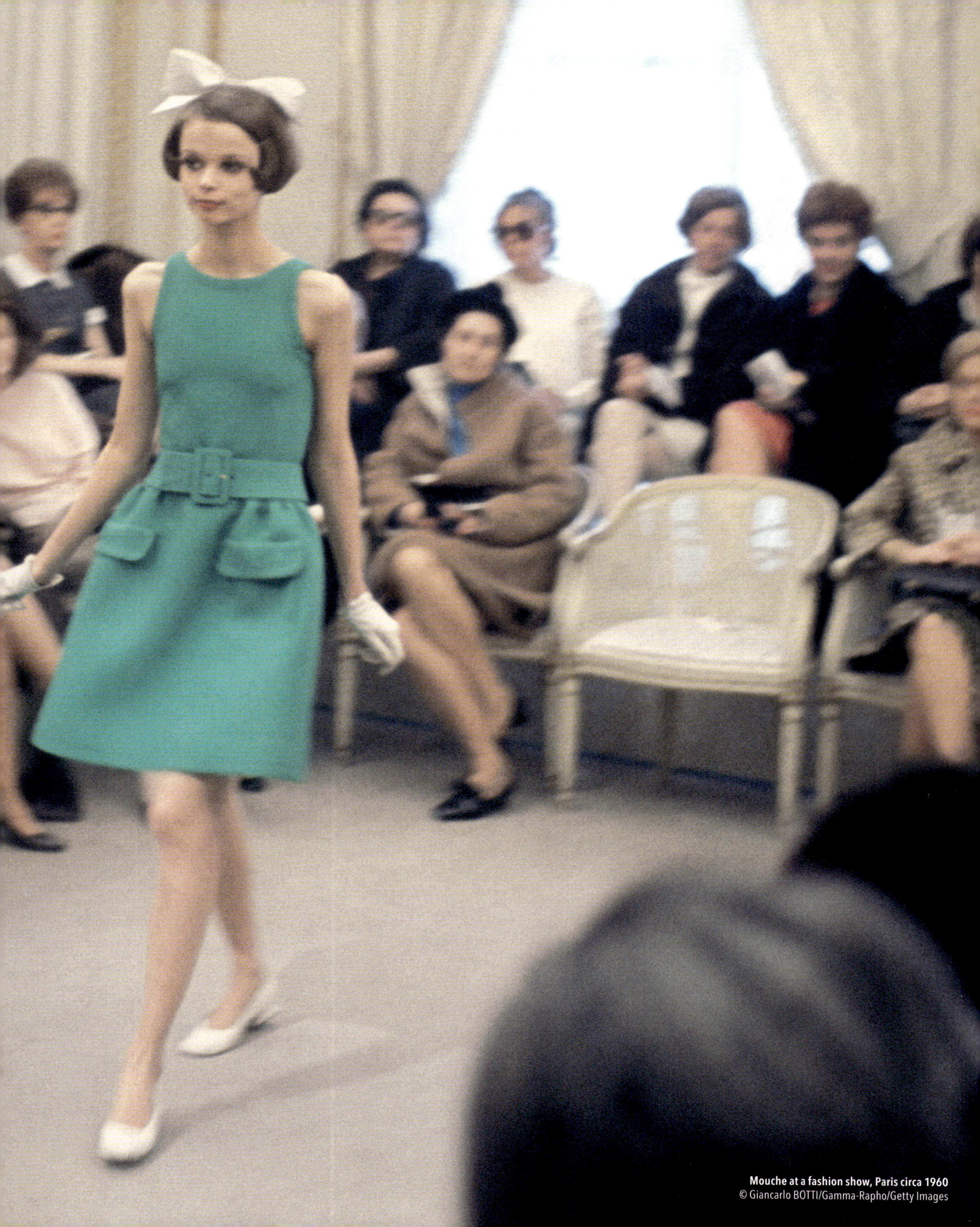

Mouche at a fashion show, Paris circa 1960
© Giancarlo BOTTI/Gamma-Rapho/Getty Images

Peggy Moffitt is the quintessential mod model. One of the most recognizable figures of the 1960s' fashion scene, she also immortalized the Pop Art aesthetic. Her prolific work as both muse and collaborator of Rudi Gernreich produced an archive of timeless images that serves to define the modernity and ingenuity of the late midcentury modern era. Peggy Moffitt did not simply model clothes; she embodied them. With her heightened use of accessories, blunt asymmetrical bowl cut created by Vidal Sassoon, and extreme Kabuki-inspired makeup, she elevated fashion to the plane of performance art. Her innovative use of pigments and liquid liner, combined with the precision of her application, transformed the landscape of beauty. Peggy approached makeup from the point of view of a fine artist, incorporating mediums and techniques beyond the makeup palette, creating looks that were multidimensional and emotionally evocative. Peggy's makeup skills broke boundaries, as she made of herself a means to shock and inspire.

Peggy was a bridge between the worlds of modeling and the avant-garde. Self-expression and the cultivation of nonconformist ideals of beauty is Peggy's art form. It is what defines her as both a beauty icon and a fashion legend.

Pat McGrath

Photography by William Claxton

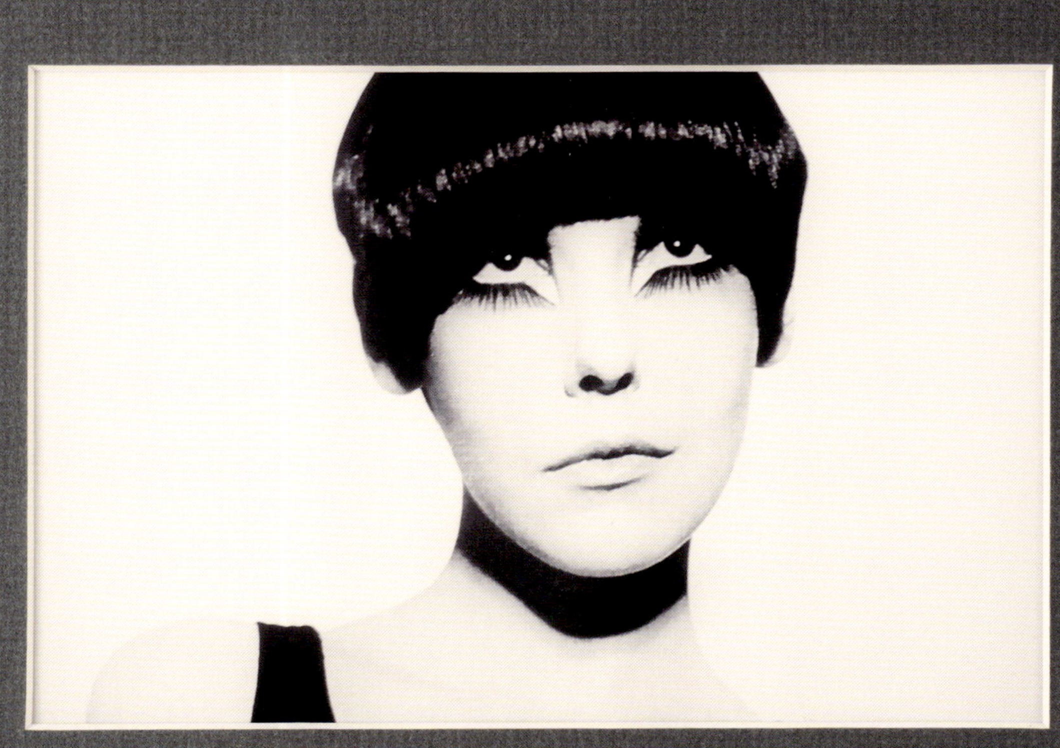

Capucine

I first encountered Capucine when I was home from school with a fever, watching movies on television. The film that most captivated me that day was *The Pink Panther*. Everyone in America, it seemed, knew both the theme song and the eponymous cartoon cat from the opening credits. But I'd never heard of the ravishing, exquisitely dressed creature who played Peter Sellers's adulterous wife. No cinema star I had ever seen could compare to this soignée vision with the aquiline nose, intelligent eyes, lush mouth, cosmopolitan accent, and—this made her even more unreal—flawless comic timing.

Capucine embodies a moment when the aspiration of young people was to look, dress, and behave in a poised, polished, and sophisticated way, rather than remain juveniles forever. Capucine was at most thirty-four when she made that film, but her mannerisms, demeanor, and wardrobe were those of a mature woman of the world. If such an actress could be found today, she would be cast as a villain. Like her close colleague Audrey Hepburn, Capucine was an intimate of Hubert de Givenchy, for whom she modeled. Capucine resembled an illustration by Givenchy's friend René Gruau come to life. I don't know why there weren't more actresses like her, in Hollywood or elsewhere, and I regret that models don't move and speak, much less look, like her anymore.

Capucine's patrician beauty was so preternatural that the late Hollywood man-about-town Richard Gully, Jack Warner's confidant and special assistant, shared with me fascinating rumors that Capucine was actually a man. This canard about her is understandable, because Capucine's otherworldly appearance resists categories, and also because Capucine possessed the kind of hyperfemininity and deadly wit that is often associated with drag queens. Gully also said Capucine killed herself because she didn't want to age; she was just sixty-two and appeared remarkably unchanged. It is a simplistic explanation, as Capucine was a manic-depressive. But if it is even partly true, Capucine succeeded in preserving her peerless, perfect elegance eternally.

Amy Fine Collins

Photography by Georges Dambier

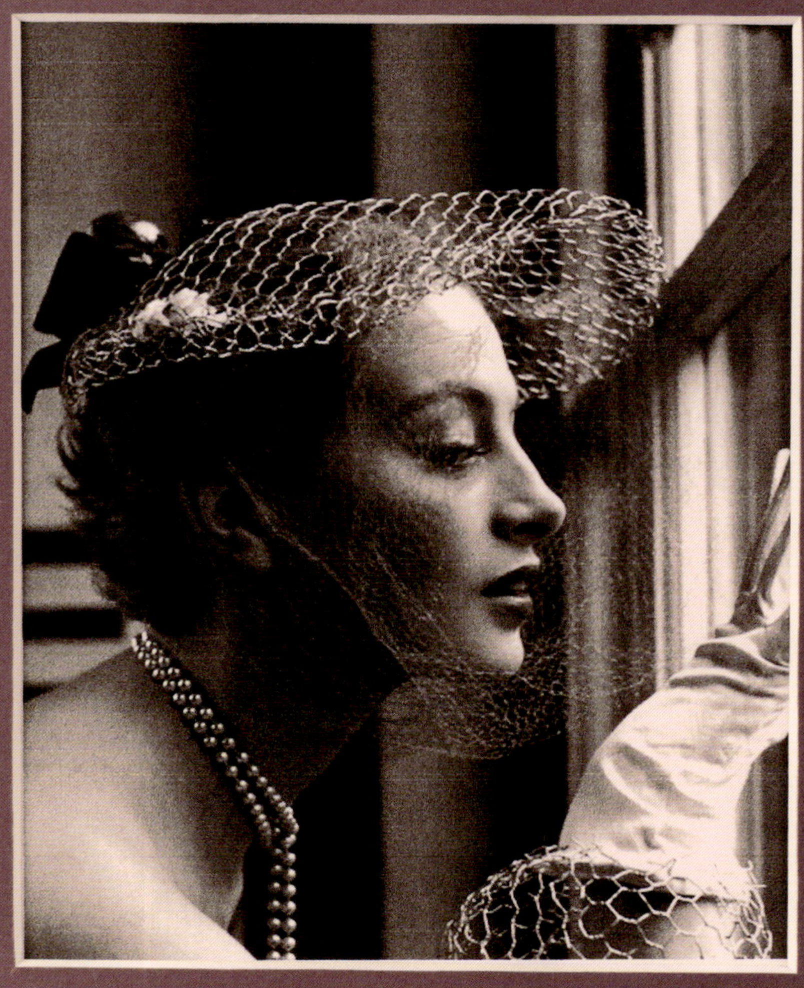

Capucine

Susan Moncur

Were it not for the uniformity and elegance of her features, and the imperceptible awkwardness which, I believe, led her to hesitate before every move and, paradoxically, achieve ultimate perfection, Susan's exceptional sensitivity would go unnoticed in the outside world. Because it was in the studio—as soon as she stepped into the changing room and the transubstantiation took place—that Susan showed her perceptive genius. Under the lens, she captured the impalpable, revealing the secrets of her great beauty and of her pain, which seemed to go hand in hand. I see a parallel with myself—but enough of me.

With the exception of NASA (and perhaps also the Lord Himself), nothing and no one else on earth can lay claim to this quality. If Susan were to close her eyes, darkness would fall on the world.

Serge Lutens

Photography by Serge Lutens

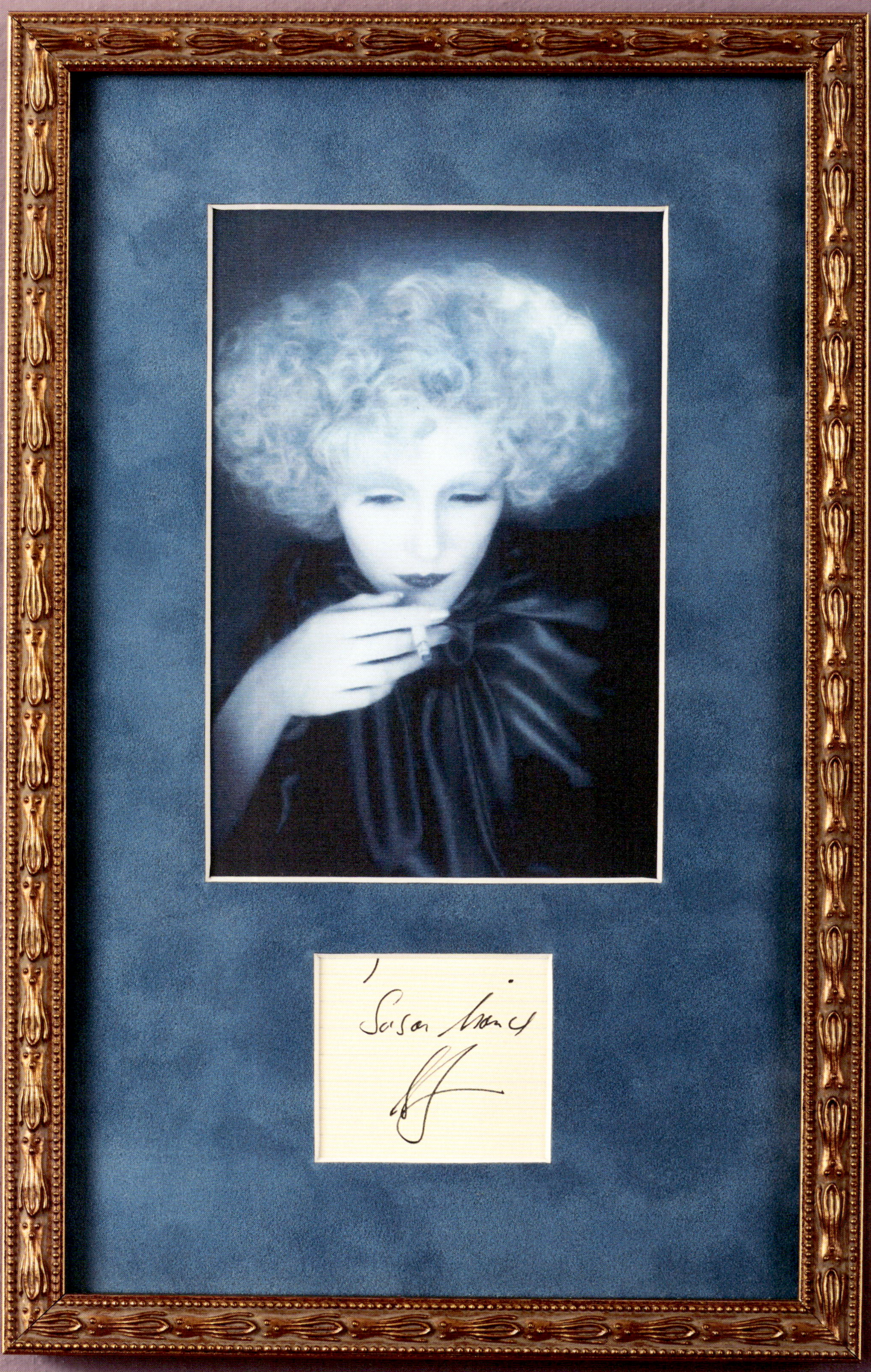

Princess Elizabeth of Toro
lawyer model actress and

Diplomat... she is beyond definition

a quality had by few but so necessary
to live to traverse across this complex world
and she traverses brilliantly

necessary and important to oppose the onslaught of
many many classifications attached to women
that inhibit and diminish our lives

that is why Elizabeth of Toro is an ideal to aspire to

Adrienne Kennedy

Photography by Irving Penn

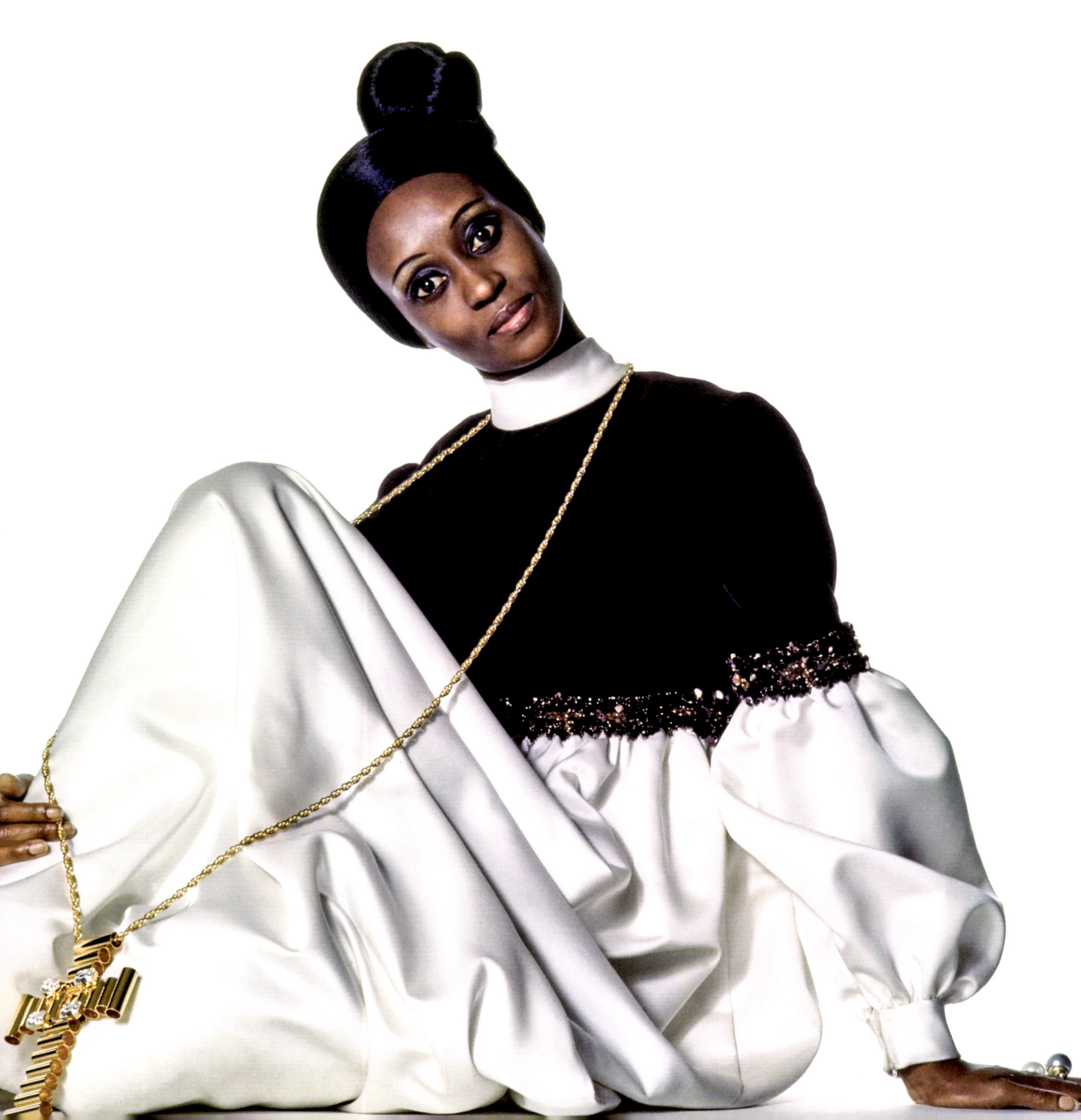

Inès was the most extraordinary French model because she had that
thing the others didn't have: elegance with attitude!

Karl Lagerfeld

Photography by Karl Lagerfeld

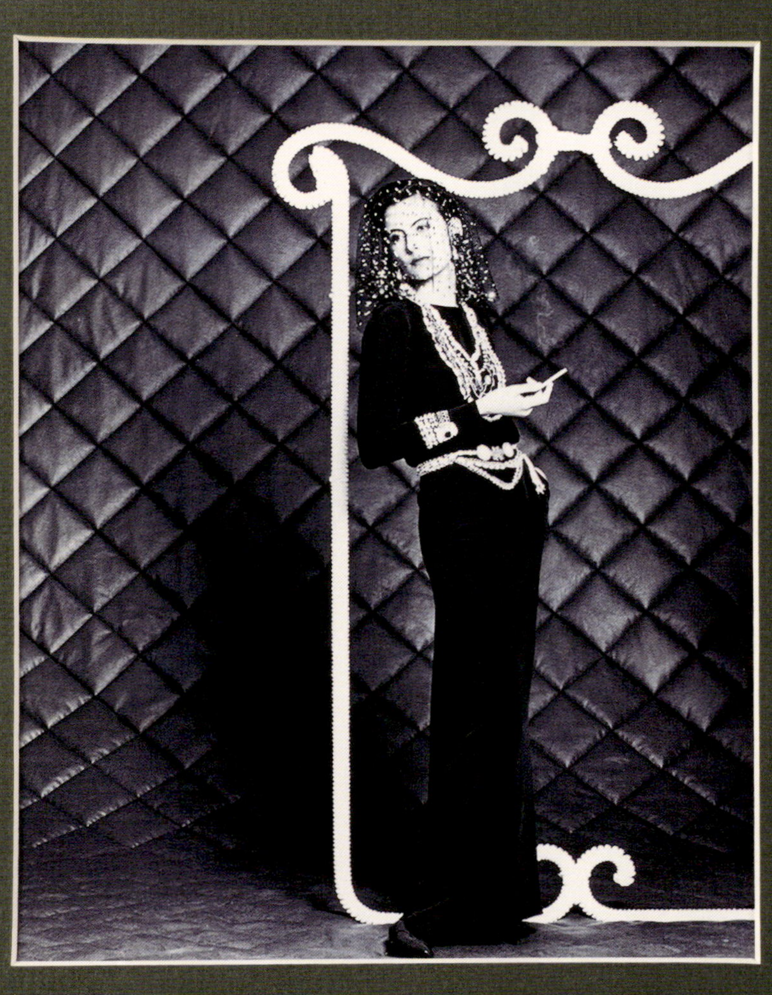
Pour Christopher,
Mille Baisers,
Inès

Anh Duong

The first impression (slightly falsified by time, maybe, but not by much). A young and proper demoiselle in a well-to-do-little-girl outfit: a high-waisted navy blue peacoat, a Breton hat worn on the back of her head, chin-length hair worn loose or in a ponytail, dark stockings, patent leather ballet flats, and a handbag resembling a lunchbox that she would hold in front of her with both hands. A face like an Egyptian or Khmer bas-relief, wearing an indefinable glare and smile. Sent to me by a friend from Hermès, or by Marie Seznec, she waited for me in the old-fashioned, beige salon of Jean Patou on the rue Saint-Florentin in the early 1980s.

We were looking for a new girl for the "pose," back in the days when a couture house presented its collection to clients a few times a week. I hired her on the spot, or almost; this unexpected apparition was such a pretty contrast to the creatures in vogue at the time, whose looks were tinted by disco, aerobics, *Dynasty*, or *Dallas*.

She was always a little absent. She barely spoke during the fittings, but you knew she had her own opinion. I realized much later that during these silent and still moments she was observing, scrutinizing, making notes of it all, her eyes like lasers. One day, by chance, I discovered that she had a talent for drawing caricatures. Her rare remarks were surprisingly light: tongue-in-cheek humor, paradoxically eccentric beneath the Zen exterior. This hieratism tinged with nonchalance, this haughty and charming irony, allowed me to dress her in outfits that required unshakable composure. She made me bold. Nothing scared her; she would wear the most audacious garments as if she was taking a bet: a gray-pink mink pencil skirt, a mini crinoline of deep red ostrich feathers, a top hat shaped like a peanut, drapings that you would see on the dukes of Bourgogne, a Hollywoodish sari, or an evening gown of mauve swan feathers.

Fashion back then was theatrical, operatic. We were living in an era of insouciant frivolity and modernity, but looking nostalgically back to the extravagant *raffinements* and sharp spirit of the years between 1930 and 1960. Thi Anh (her full name, which she used then) had that extravagant elegance, a natural sophistication in all circumstances—an idio-syncratic, contemporary sense of glamour, of Parisian chic. And, season after season, she revealed an undeniable talent for interpretation. The interplay between the outfits she wore and her strong personality, as expressed in gestures, poses, looks, or mimicry, soon fascinated the press.

She was part of the team that came with me from Jean Patou when I founded the house of Christian Lacroix. The impact of our first show, in July 1987, was due to Thi Anh and Marie Seznec: a sumptuous and spiritual duet of naughty girls, mischievous minxes, snobbish but funny *précieuses*. They had gotten to know each other well at the rue Saint-Florentin, and their complicity was at its peak. They improvised and challenged each other with coquettish poses. I still have visions of Thi Anh on that runway: turning her wrist or lifting her chin, throwing sidelong looks at the audience, making small gestures to show an evening bag. She was my drawings come to life, interpreting their lines, their contortions, their insolent allure, their prissiness. When this high bohemia collection, and the ones that followed it, went on the road to Los Angeles and New York, Thi Anh was the ambassadress of our traveling troupe. One day she decided to stay behind, where other worlds, other roles, and other lives were waiting for her.

About ten years later I found her again, in downtown New York, an impeccable hostess and an admired painter, now known simply as Anh Duong. The satirical drawings of the rue Saint-Florentin had become giant canvases, impressive and overwhelming self-portraits, paintings of the flesh, of fabrics, and of the soul (the ingredients of couture as well as theater).

What a beautiful journey from the rue Saint-Florentin and the faubourg Saint-Honoré to where she is now, after several novel-like lives. A rare trajectory, personal and precious, unlike many of our contemporaries, who ended up joining the fold. She has nothing to do with those socialites, those ordinary jet-setters. We should invent a new word for her, something that synthesizes the lionesses of the 1890s, the queens of café society between the wars, and the bright young things of the Twenties. Delicate, but unflinchingly anchored in reality.

Christian Lacroix

Photography by Steven Meisel

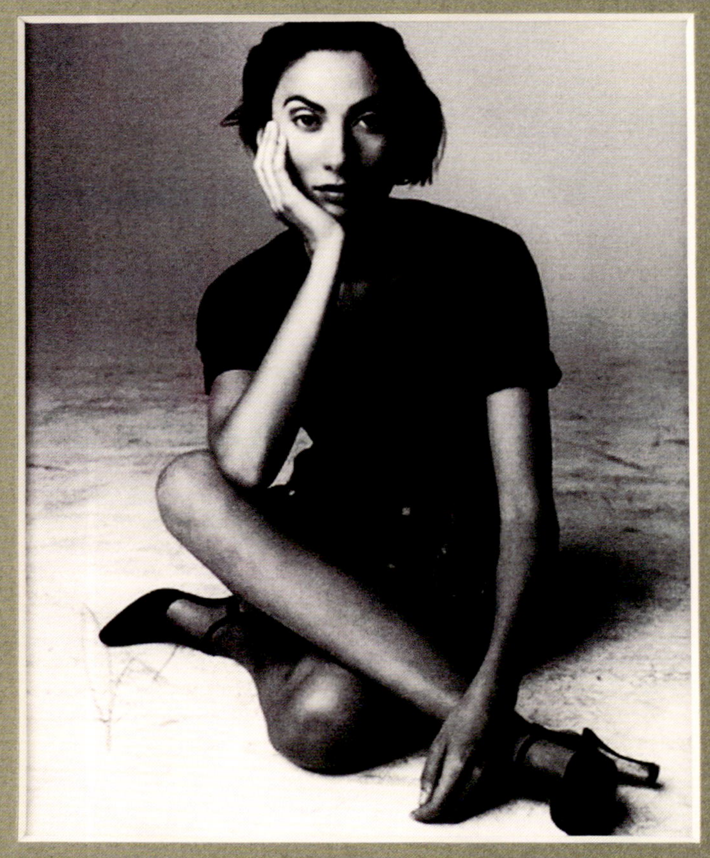

Betty Perske was a young actress who modeled just long enough to pose in front of a sign for the American Red Cross Blood Donor Service on the cover of a wartime issue of *Harper's Bazaar*. At eighteen, her hair parted on the left, one eyebrow raised in a critical circumflex, she was already a skeptical, elegant presence. The photo set off a chain reaction that led to the director Howard Hawks changing her name to Lauren Bacall and casting her in *To Have and Have Not* opposite Humphrey Bogart, whom she soon married. Bogie and Bacall became legend.

In 1952, for *How to Marry a Millionaire*, Bacall's long femme-fatale-in-génue locks were cut into the chin-length wave that became the basis of her adult style. The contrast between that brisk blonde wave and the feline seduction of her features sealed her allure as the embodiment of sophistication. Many changed their name—the first, or the last—to Lauren, to partake of that allure. No longer a fashion model, she became a model for fashion.

Humphrey Bogart died in 1957, and Betty Bacall moved to New York, to a vast apartment facing Central Park where mahogany moldings outlined every feature of every room. A widow at thirty-two, the mother of two children, Stephen and Leslie, she married the actor Jason Robards, had another son, Sam, divorced, and never stopped acting. Often, the Broadway plays she starred in, such as *Applause* and *Woman of the Year*, relied on the charge of elegant class that she brought with her. In 1968, she starred in a television preview of the Paris collections called *Bacall and the Boys*—the boys being Yves Saint Laurent, Emmanuel Ungaro, Marc Bohan, and Pierre Cardin. The poster rendered the blonde wave above a hot-pink turtleneck jumpsuit, in Joe Eula's famous scribble.

In a 1953 episode of *What's My Line?*, Bacall was the mystery guest; the players, eyes masked, had to guess who she was. Wearing a dress with a single sleeve, she sat close to the host, as fluid and eager as a cat longing to be petted; to disguise her voice, she answered every question in French. They guessed her identity anyway.

Betty loved Paris; she loved clothes and people, her children and Democratic politics; she loved dogs and paintings of dogs, Renaissance furniture and tiny Ashanti bronze weights and gold chains and watch fobs and pendants and beige and cashmere sweaters. She wheeled baby Sam through Central Park in midwinter, her ankles bare above her loafers. She shopped, a lot, punctuated her conversation with "Oh my nerves!" and "It's a disaster!", and said, "Work is the most important thing—it's the only thing you have that's yours." When she was eighty-eight, her looks dissolved by time, her hair no longer able to wave, she still had the circumflex eyebrows that said, "Prove it."

Joan Juliet Buck

Photography by Philipe Halsman

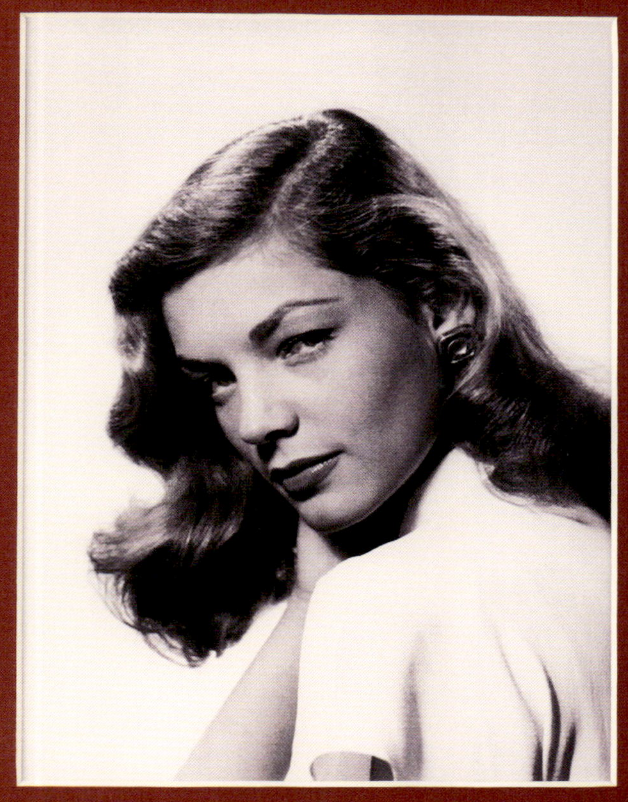

Veruschka is the most beautiful woman in the world. There's just nobody like her. If she's beautiful, she's beautiful alone. Veruschka's bones, her body, her extraordinary length have compelled her to invent her own person. There's just no one she could imitate.

Veruschka is the only woman I permit to look at herself in the mirror while I'm photographing her. The mirror makes most women aware of their weaknesses and, in trying to correct them, they come up with evasions, hiding arms that seem too thin or hips that seem too wide. Veruschka knows that it is what's peculiar to her that's beautiful and she works to bring it forward. It's wonderful to see her searching for and emphasizing her irregularities.

There are times during a sitting when she turns to look at me, or at the camera, and, without so much as lifting an eyebrow or curving her mouth, smiles, challenges. It's like the opposite of the Dylan song, "I'll let you in my dream if you'll let me in yours." That seems to be what most people need. But not Veruschka. She'll let you look into her dream but she wouldn't fit in yours.

Richard Avedon

Photography by Richard Avedon

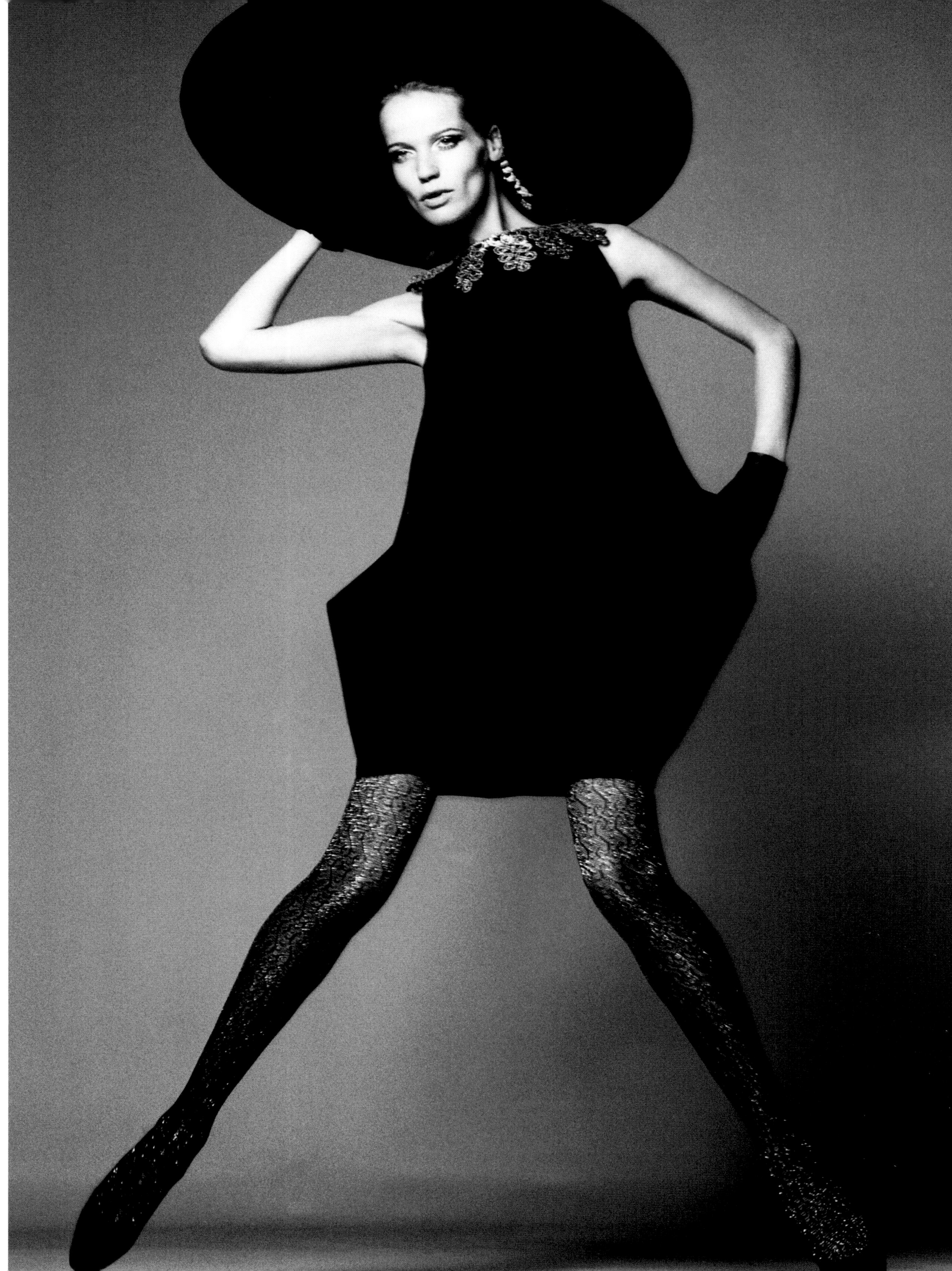

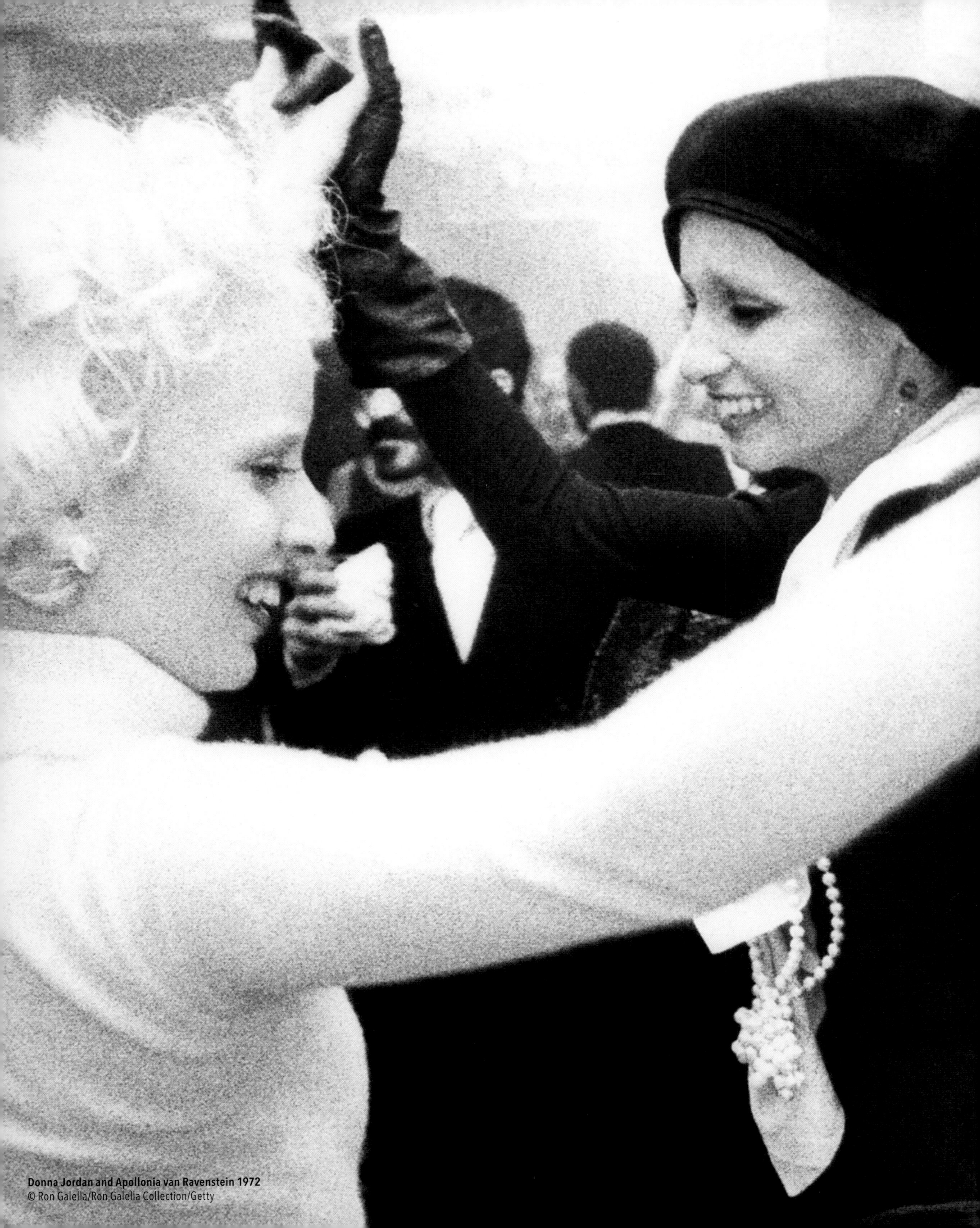

Donna Jordan and Apollonia van Ravenstein 1972
© Ron Galella/Ron Galella Collection/Getty

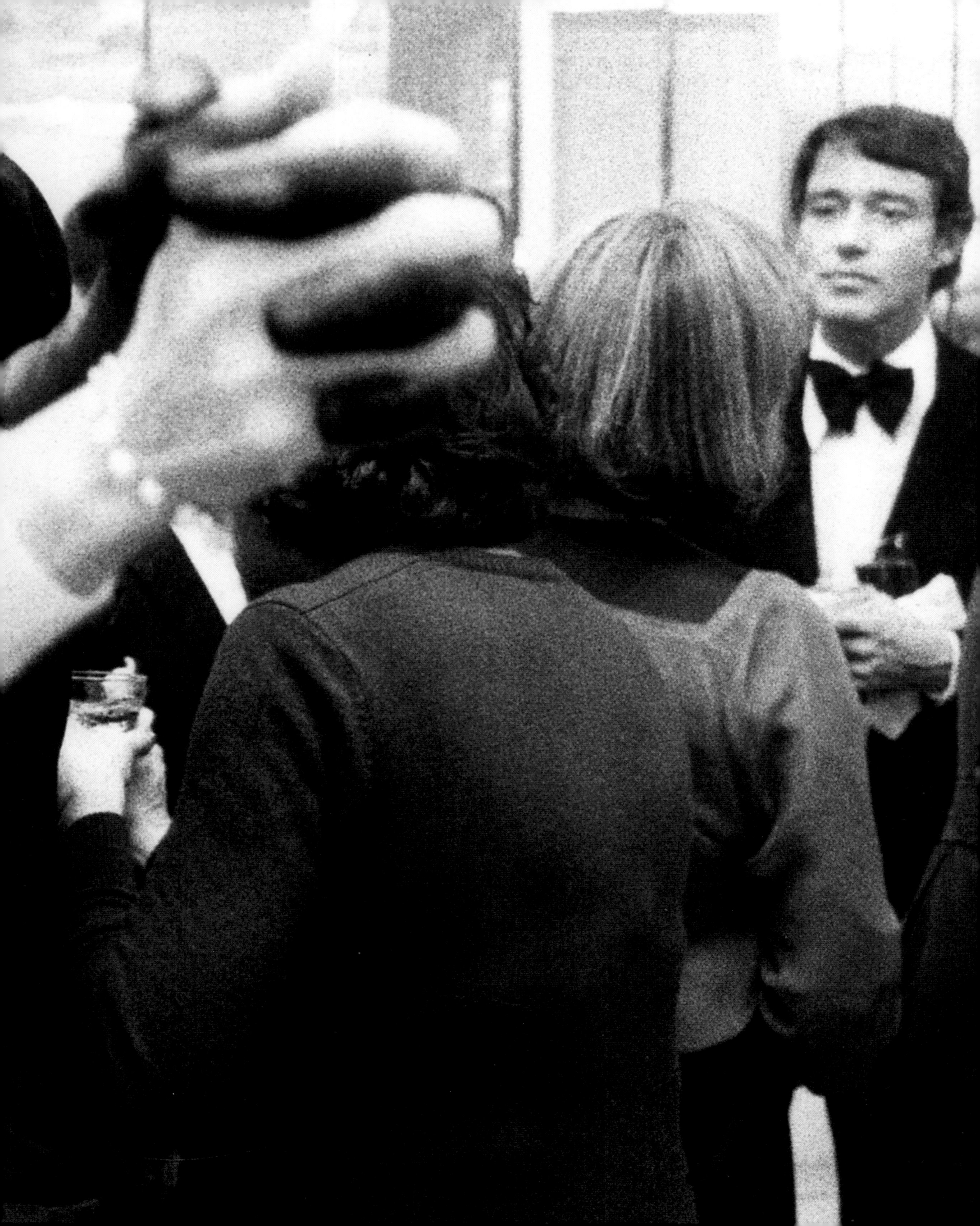

China Machado

I remember vividly the first time I saw a China Machado photograph. It was 1993; I was fourteen or fifteen years old. I opened Richard Avedon's *An Autobiography* and was captivated by one image in particular: a shot of a model wearing a Fifties suit and a weird high chignon. I don't know exactly why I was so mesmerized by that image. There was the hand, the parallel between the model's index finger and the cigarette she was holding—a finger that looked like a very sophisticated claw. And the sharp cheekbones, the almond-bright eyes. But above all, I was drawn by her half smile, a mix of pride and defiance. I read the credits and saw that the photo was taken in 1958, and the model's name was China Machado.

China Machado: what a mysterious name, I thought. Even thirty-five years after the photograph was taken, that woman looked like no model I'd seen before. So China *caught* me. In the years that followed, every time I saw her name or her face in a magazine, I paid attention. (My "discovery" was long before Google.) That's how I learned that China was a pioneer: her undeniable beauty broke the rules about what a model should look like. Her magic was the result of a mix of ethnicities: her mother, who was from Macau, met her father, who was from Portugal, in Hong Kong. Little China grew up in Buenos Aires. As an adult, she had a relationship with the famous Spanish bullfighter Luis Miguel Dominguin. I refuse to call these details "exotic," but I dare to bet that they made China's career.

I love the story behind that Avedon image. *Harper's Bazaar* refused to publish it because China didn't fit their idea of a model, and Avedon refused to renew his contract with the magazine if the image wasn't published. The publisher backed down. And so a longtime friendship between photographer and model was sealed. China was photographed by Avedon exclusively for the next five years, and became a regular face in the magazine. A few years later, she became its fashion editor: poetic justice, which probably tasted like sweet revenge.

I've never been lucky enough to meet China Machado in person. Still, I sense that the spell she casts derives from something more than her amazing look; it's her attitude. She looks like a brave, strong woman. She's in her late eighties now and recently returned to modeling, in fabulous photographs by Steven Meisel and Bruce Weber, among others. In these new photos I see the same pride and defiance I saw the first time I fell in love with her.

Luis Venegas

Photography by Neal Barr

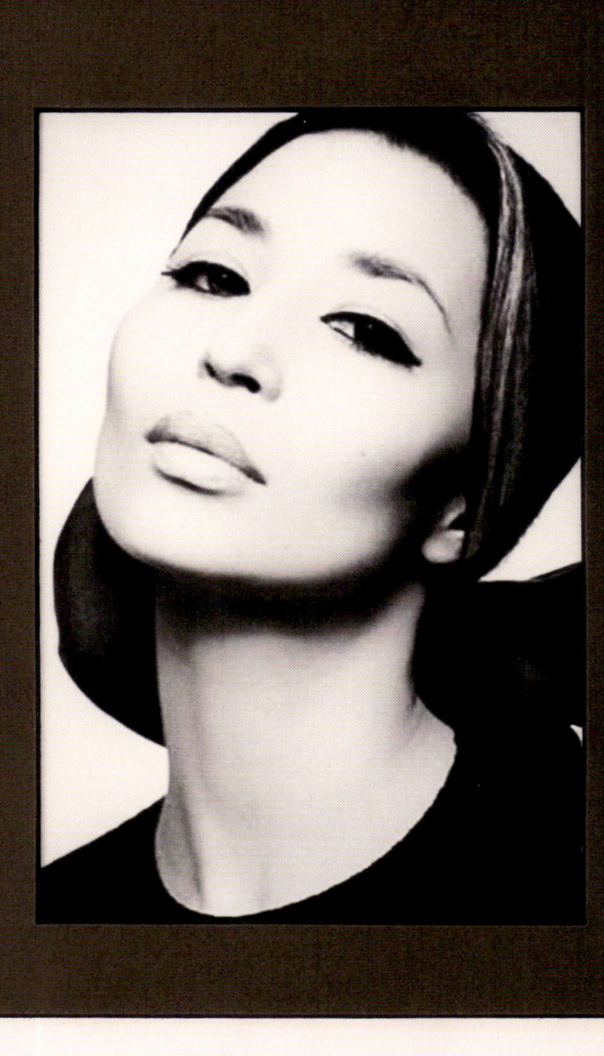

Christopher!
Hi, how nice of you!
Thank you
Chie Mori

Rene Russo

In 1981, I was booked by Revlon to do a shoot in Los Angeles with Rene
and David Leddick. When I arrived at the studio, she was sitting outside
in the bright sunlight, studying her lines. Her eyes were hooded against
the morning sun. She wore no sunglasses. She had already found her es-
cape from the world of high fashion. She had decided to be an actress.

Rene Russo was as big as you could get, at the top of the ladder. No one
had as many magazine covers or high fashion spreads as Rene Russo.
Scavullo and Avedon fought over her. Yet she was so easy to work with
that, in fact, I can't remember a thing about that particular shoot. Her
beauty was breathtaking, but she had no vanity. I'd apply makeup in the
style of the day, and she was always fine with it. Purples, reds, nothing
really natural, but makeup never overwhelmed her face.

Anytime I was booked with Rene Russo, I knew it would be a good day.

Sandy Linter

Photography by Scavullo

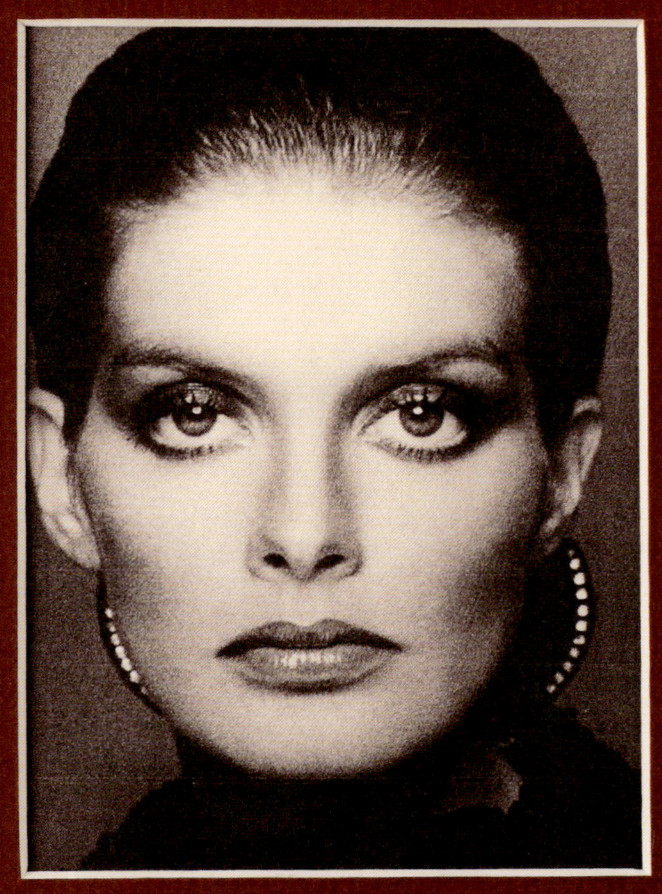

Teri Toye may not have been the first transgender model, but she was the first not to hide the fact that she was born male. Teri was a woman; her birth gender was insignificant. She was just Teri: smart, funny, sarcastic, and chic. It was a chic she learned from Steven Meisel and Stephen Sprouse, who taught her that being stripped of all the obvious trappings of femininity—heels, makeup, frilly clothes, set hair—gave her a modern edge. Teri would go out to the clubs at night in a black T-shirt worn as a dress, black opaque stockings, flats, a coat wrapped around her body and thrown off her shoulders, and sunglasses. Always sunglasses: day, night, outdoors, indoors.

In 1983, when Sprouse wanted to do his first big show outside his showroom, Teri was his fit model. She was five foot ten, reed-thin, small-busted and small-hipped, with great legs and narrow ankles. The clothes, which were downtown cool with a dash of the 1960s, made out of the most expensive fabrics and tailored impeccably, hung on her perfectly. With her long blonde hair and overgrown bangs, she was the embodiment of the new downtown cool girl. The show was done in a concert venue, not a hotel ballroom like the other fashion shows that season. There was no seating. The audience stood looking up at a stage with a wall of Fender amps and a lineup of Sprouse-dressed male models. Suddenly, violently breaking through the lineup, there was Teri—dressed in a black fake fur, black T-shirt dress, an oversized funnel fur hat, and thigh-high motorcycle boots, stomping, not sashaying, down the runway. At that moment, Sprouse became the most interesting new fashion star and Teri became the model of the moment.

Teri modeled for a few years after that show, for other designers as well as Sprouse, and in editorial shoots. Then, in 1987, she retired and moved back to Des Moines, Iowa, where she began renovating historic homes.

The year of the Sprouse show, when The Fashion Group put together their trend report for their members, the fashion show segment closed with the Stephen Sprouse collection. When Teri walked down the runway, a voice came over the PA and proclaimed her "Girl of the Year." She was!

Paul Cavaco

Photography by Steven Meisel

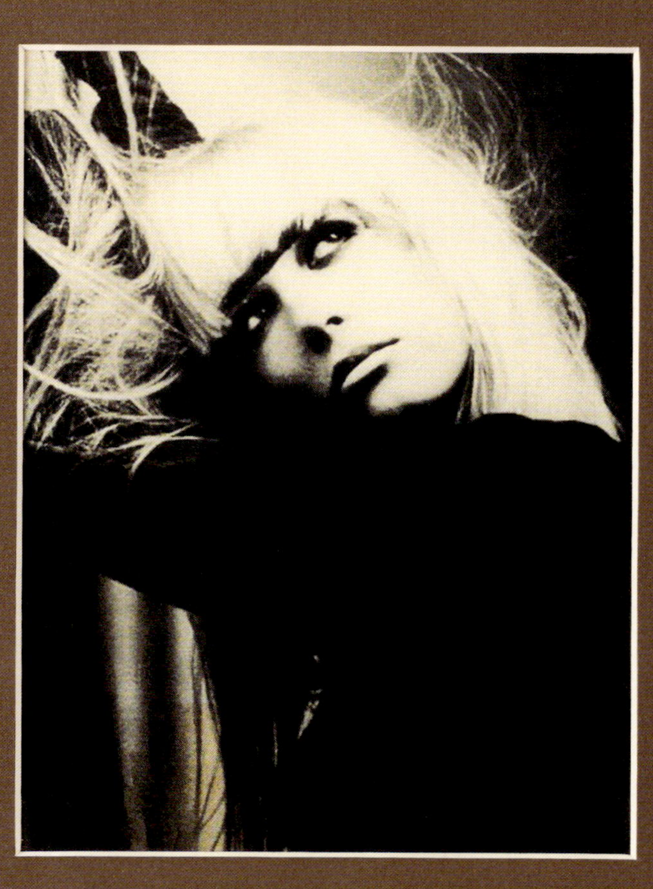
♡
T. T.

Strangely, I only met Pattie Boyd a few years ago, at Cilla Black's last party, which she gave just before she passed away. Pattie was, and is, the most beautiful dollybird I have ever seen.

In the late 1960s I nearly ran her over in front of Claridge's hotel. She was like a gazelle as she sprinted out of the way. The day was foggy, and she was wearing foggy-colored clothes. That image has remained in my head for the last forty years.

Barbara Hulanicki

Photography by David Bailey

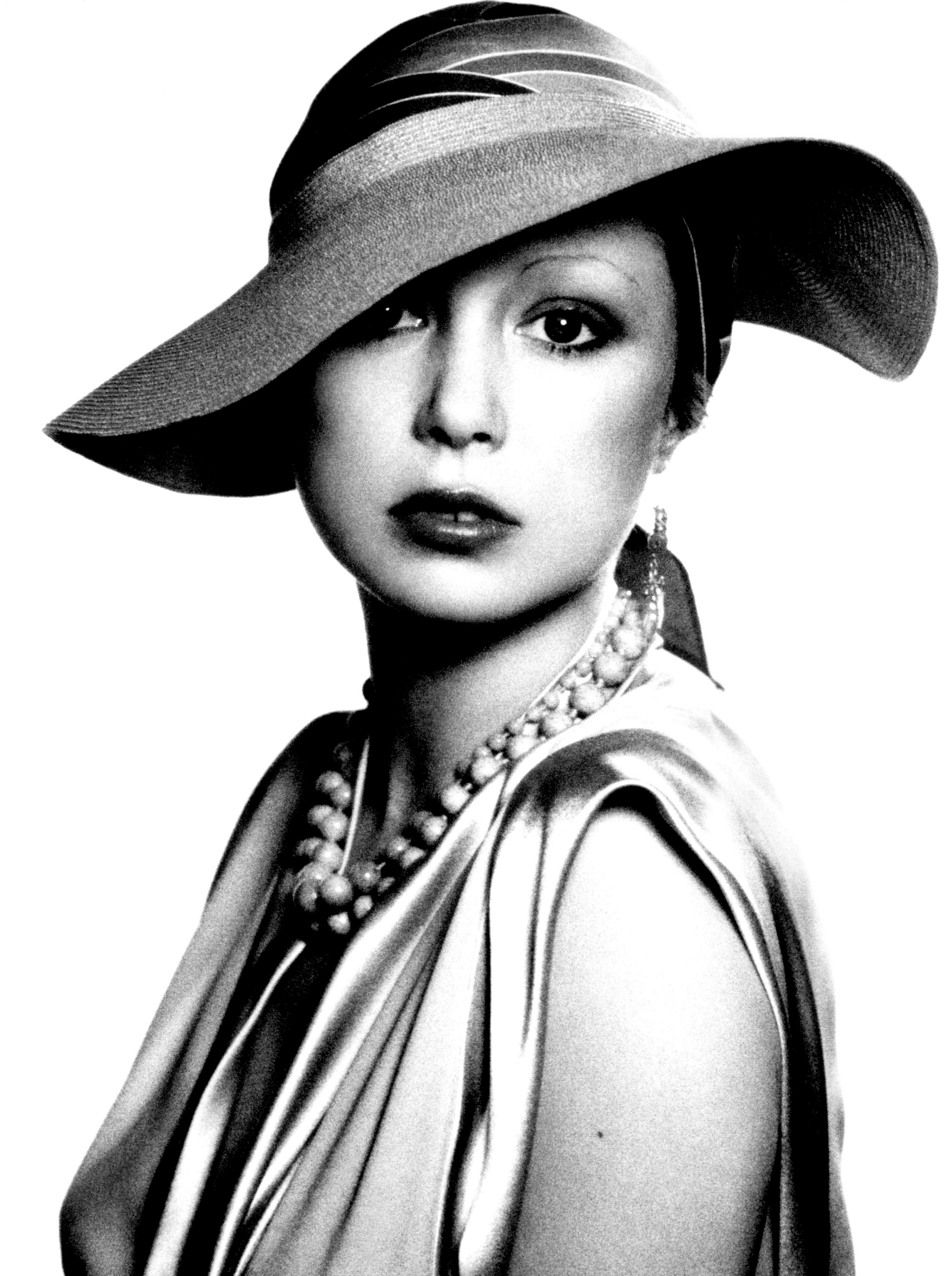

Jean Shrimpton

I first became aware of Jean Shrimpton from Yardley Slicker ads in *Seventeen* magazine. With her pink vinyl rain hat and frosted lipstick, she epitomized the London dollybird. I collected all her magazine covers: *Newsweek, Vogue, Bazaar, Glamour, McCall's.*

My mom bought me a copy of *My Own Story: The Truth about Modeling* by Jean Shrimpton. I fell in love with all the David Bailey photos, especially the one of her in the Mongolian fur coat. I read that this was Bailey's favorite too! One day I saw an ad for Yardley in the *Detroit News* saying that Jean would be at the department store J. L. Hudson's downtown. My mom drove me there to see her. I had never seen anyone so pale, so skinny, with the longest legs. I got a signed photo of her and her German shepherd.

I imagine she must have been wearing Biba. Her peasant top was gathered at the neck, and the skinny sleeves ended in huge billows, with drawstrings at the wrist. What surprised me most was her hair. In the States we were used to "Breck girl" hair, shampooed daily. But her hair was scraggly. That changed my idea of what was cool forever.

Anna Sui

Photography by Unknown

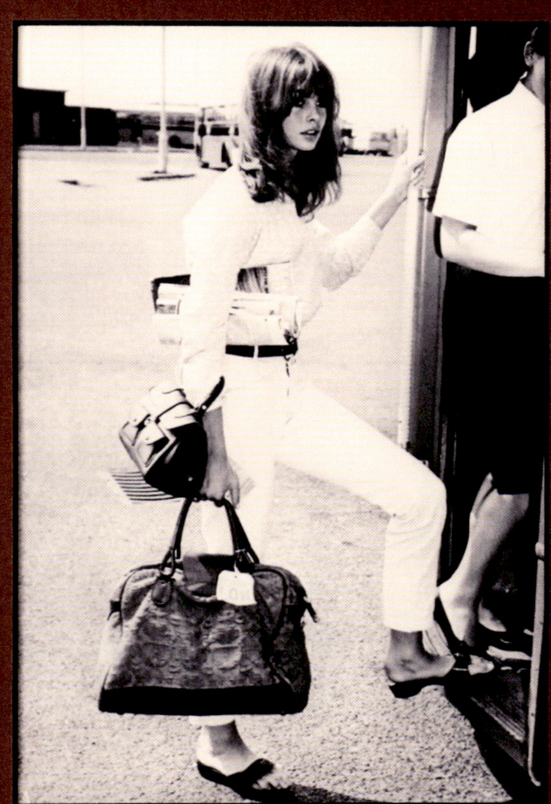

Best wishes
Jean Shrimpton

Karen, at a glimpse: a mystical crimson-haired goddess, radiant of a rose
moonlit skin. With a more resonant eye, you are curiously compelled to
sense the deeper being that exists.

Strength, awareness, brazenly witted, oozing with grace yet youth's bohemian independent free spirit, a humanitarian heart has also the intellect and knowledge of the wise tradition of song even in the most obscure.

Passion and romance in her spirit shows in her voice in song. A creative
being of gentle yet grounded originality and purpose.

Karen is light and kindness. Friendly to the letter.

Chan Marshall

Photography by Steven Meisel

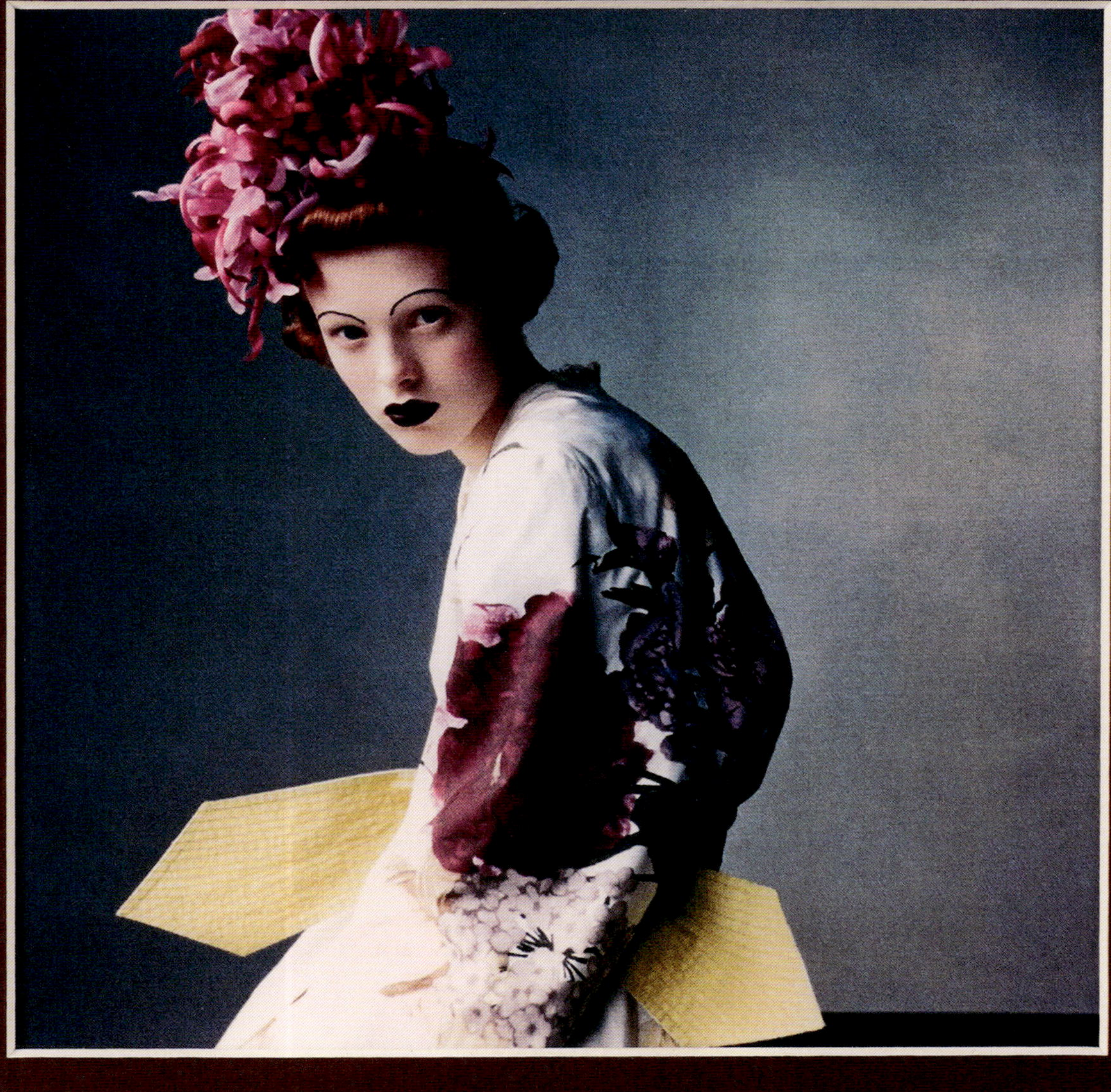

Suzy Parker

I never met Suzy Parker, the impossibly gorgeous, carrot-topped, green-eyed, freckled beauty, but I did spend a great deal of time with her estranged older sister, Dorian Leigh, who filled me in on much of Suzy's history and appeal. It was as if I knew her well, and since I was so very jealous of her—this model who captivated the hearts of photographers, advertisers, and the public with her kinetic personality— I studied her from afar, looked at each and every one of her photographs, and listened with fascination to the stories Dorian spun about her much younger sibling.

Suzy was the fourth daughter of a Texas couple who moved to New Jersey to raise their family. Born Cecilia Ann Renee Parker in 1932, she followed Dorian, born in 1917, Florian, born in 1918, and Georgia Bell, born in 1919. All four girls were beautiful, graceful, and talented, and although Dorian too was successful and celebrated, gracing more than fifty-six magazine covers in her career, she was neither as influential nor as natural a model as her sister. Dorian was considered "a Sargent," whereas Suzy was always known as Suzy.

Suzy paved the way for the supermodel generation. It was she who changed the photography session from a "sitting" to a "shoot." Under her influence, the great Richard Avedon's style of fashion photography evolved from static to vibrant.

At five foot ten, she set the standard for models to come: statuesque, radiant, curvy but thin, long-limbed and high-cheekboned. She joined Ford Models in 1947, aged fifteen, and was an instant hit with advertisers, fashion editors, and designers, including Coco Chanel. Her face appeared on more than seventy magazine covers, and then in films and television shows. Her acting career, too, encouraged other models to do more than just pose for photos.

For me Suzy's real legacy is that of role model and leader, breaking glass ceilings in jobs that were difficult, demanding, and frequently heart-breaking. And remember, Suzy's photographs were mostly taken before the days of digital alteration, so what you see is what was there. Amazing!

Martha Stewart

Photography by Georges Dambier

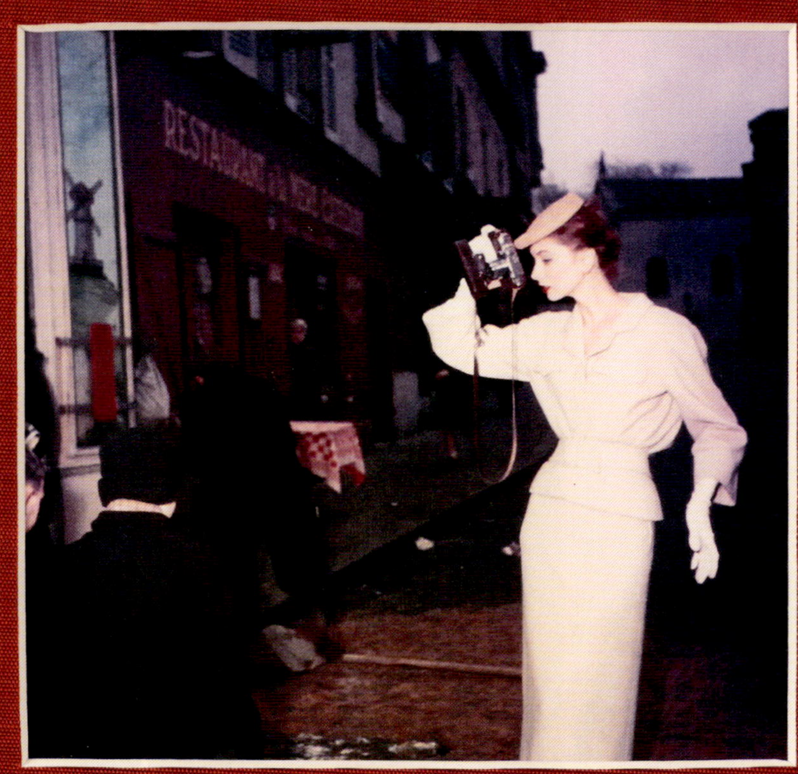

♡ Suzy Parker

Naomi Campbell is God's unique gift to humankind. Her light shines from that higher power that dwells beyond the stars! When you see Naomi, strutting, in her personal glide, you love. You feel love, God's love.

Naomi changes everything and she becomes an Ode to Joy. The light that dwells beyond the stars. She illumines from within: a soaring spirit, a tower, a wonder. In her buttery, beautiful, tantalizing black is beautiful uniqueness. She rises.

André Leon Talley

Photography by Steven Meisel

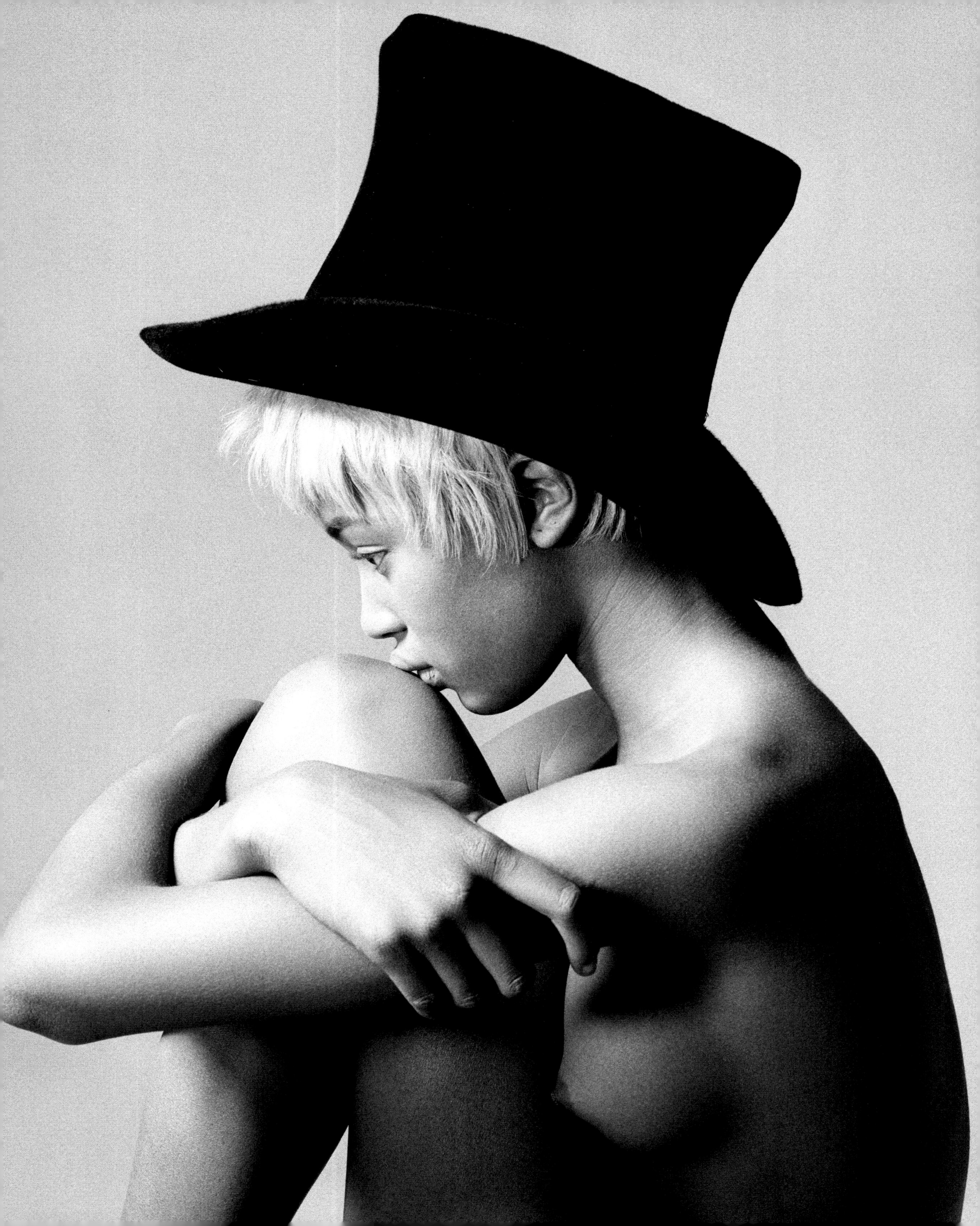

I was born in 1966, a year after her. In 1980, when she was discovered in one of those twists of fate young girls dream of, I was fourteen years old: an uncertain age, an age of fantasies, an age for icons. Paulina became one of them. I grew up following her metamorphosis. Her name, foreign but recognizable, so close to the ordinary names I knew, gave her a regal mystery.

In 1984, I graduated from high school, while she became the first Eastern European girl to appear on the cover of *Sports Illustrated*. I accumulated small jobs, one of which was modeling. I dreamed of a successful career, but deep down knew I would never be Paulina—or Carla, Karen, Christy, Linda...

In 1988, with her record-breaking Estée Lauder contract, this kid from Czechoslovakia became the symbol of American beauty. Uptown. Caucasian. Perfect. In other photos, I'd see her with her rock 'n roll husband, with a denim jacket and crooked teeth. That same year, I had to take a corporate job and start living in the real world.

Three years later, Jennie Livingston's extraordinary documentary on the gay, black, transvestite, and transsexual community *Paris Is Burning* came out. One of the protagonists, who has given himself the name Octavia Saint Laurent, admits that he dreams only of her. Behind him, his bedroom wall is covered in posters of models—mostly Paulina. And this is how a young woman who was left to be raised by her grandparents when her parents escaped to Sweden during the Prague Spring became the symbol of the capitalist, democratic, liberal values of the West. A condensed piece of history.

Virginie Mouzat

Photography by Skrebneski

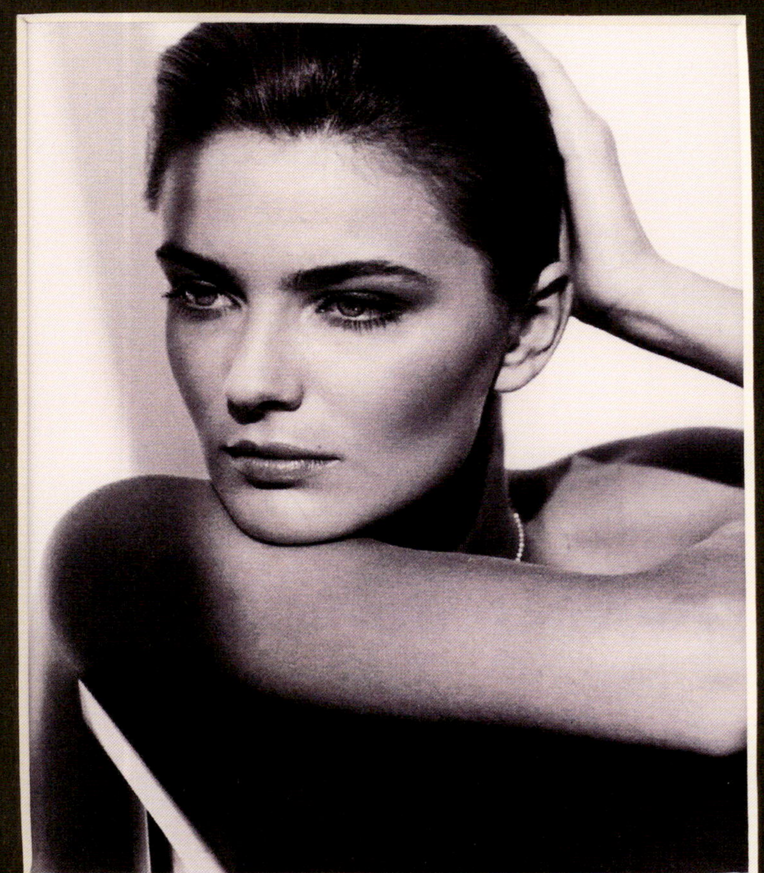

Paulina Porizkova

When the bombs rained down on London town, I was lucky enough to be evacuated to Boxwood Manor, home of the writer J. B. Priestley, and I saw another way of life, very different from the austere, monochrome landscape of two-up-two-down houses smelling of gas and boiled cabbage that I left behind. For a decade, London struggled to shake off the bleakness of postwar deprivation; then finally, there was a buzz in the air. For lively London lads like me, the world was our oyster.

When I first met Lesley Hornby through my brother Tony, who worked with her sister in a Queensway hairdresser's shop, I saw all the ingredients of a fresh new look for fashion. The Beatles had already had an enormous effect on the younger generation, who no longer felt they had to dress like their parents, but the fashion world was still run according to the dictates of the upper class, with elegant, haughty models, many of whom married into the peerage. (For example, Bronwyn Pugh, whom I adored, became Lady Astor.)

The first thing was to change her name. A beautiful emerging model, Jean Shrimpton, was known as "the Shrimp"; so, with help from my brother Tony and the brilliant photographer Barry Lategan, Lesley metamorphosed into Twiggy, a soubriquet that suited her admirably. From then on, we planned her career meticulously. I was very selective in whom I would let photograph her. In America we worked with Richard Avedon, Mel Sokolsky, and my dear friend Bert Stern. I was Bert's biggest fan, having been enormously influenced by his brilliant, innovative film *Jazz on a Summer's Day*. We also worked often with the great but underrated Carmen Schiavone.

In all honesty, it was America that made Twiggy. There's an old adage in England, especially in the music business, that if you don't crack America you haven't really made it. We did have a major success in England, after Leonard (of Mayfair!—the stomping ground of the upper class) cut Twiggy's hair in that magical little bob; when we first left for America, there were nine factories trying to cope with the demand for "Twiggy dresses," which were designed by two art students I'd recruited from the Royal College of Art. (Incidentally, the Royal College of Art was a huge influence on art and fashion at the time, with David Hockney and Peter Blake both alumni of the Sixties.) Fashion, suddenly, was for working boys and girls; it was no longer the haute couture of the upper classes. Barbara Hulanicki, with her label BIBA, kick-started the change by catering for the girl in the street, who could now afford to buy fashionable clothes. Twiggy admired Barbara greatly—and became the face of the new fashion scene.

It was Erté, the famous fashion illustrator of the 1920s and 1930s, who suggested that Twiggy should star in *The Boyfriend*. Twiggy and I had taken him to see the stage musical, thinking he'd enjoy the 1920s setting. We had actually turned down many films at that point, as I thought they weren't right for her image, but this was perfect. It took me a couple of years to find the right director, and I settled at last on Ken Russell.

Twiggy won two Golden Globe Awards, and America was at her feet.

Justin de Villeneuve

Photography by Terry Fincher

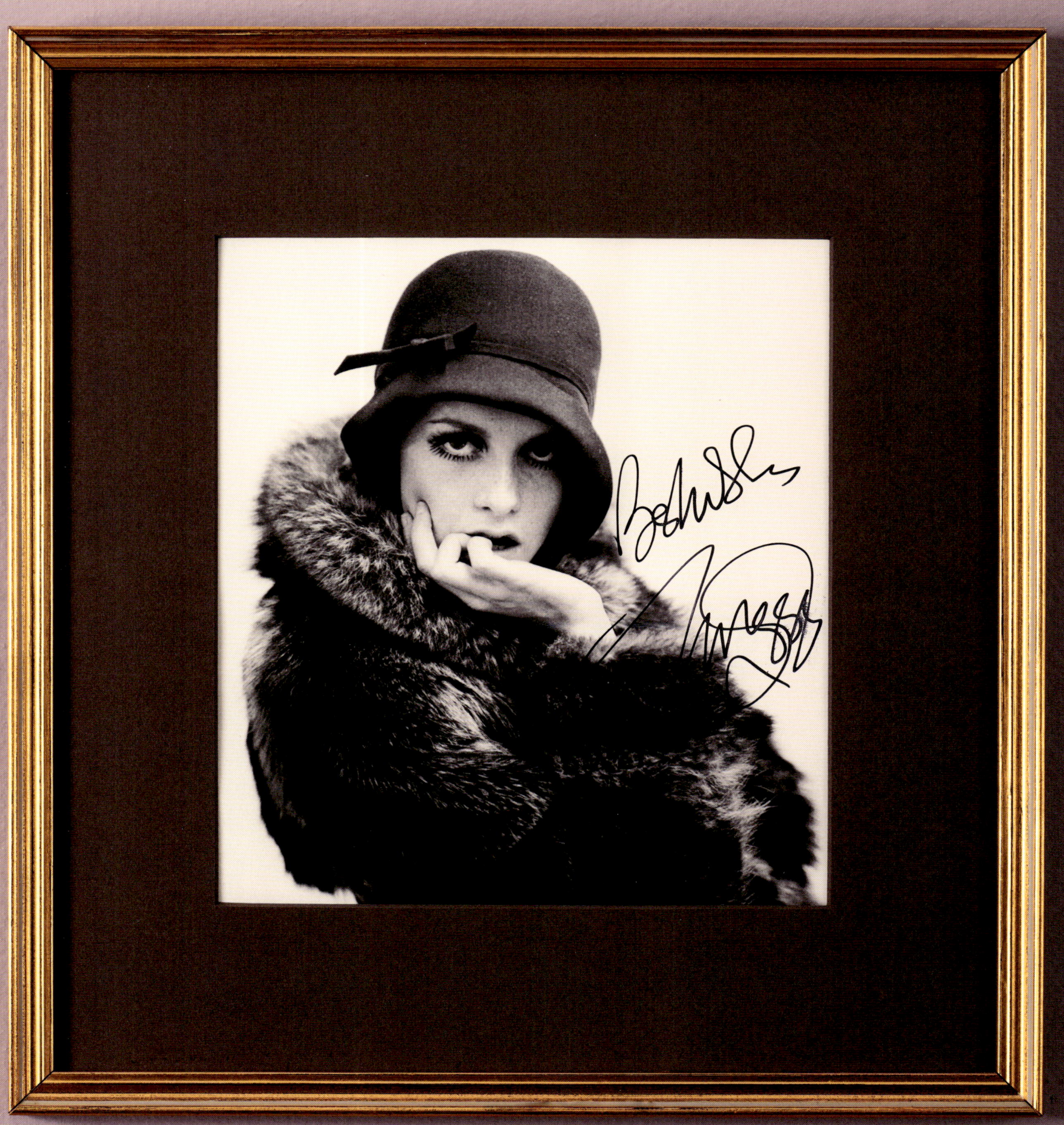
Best Wishes

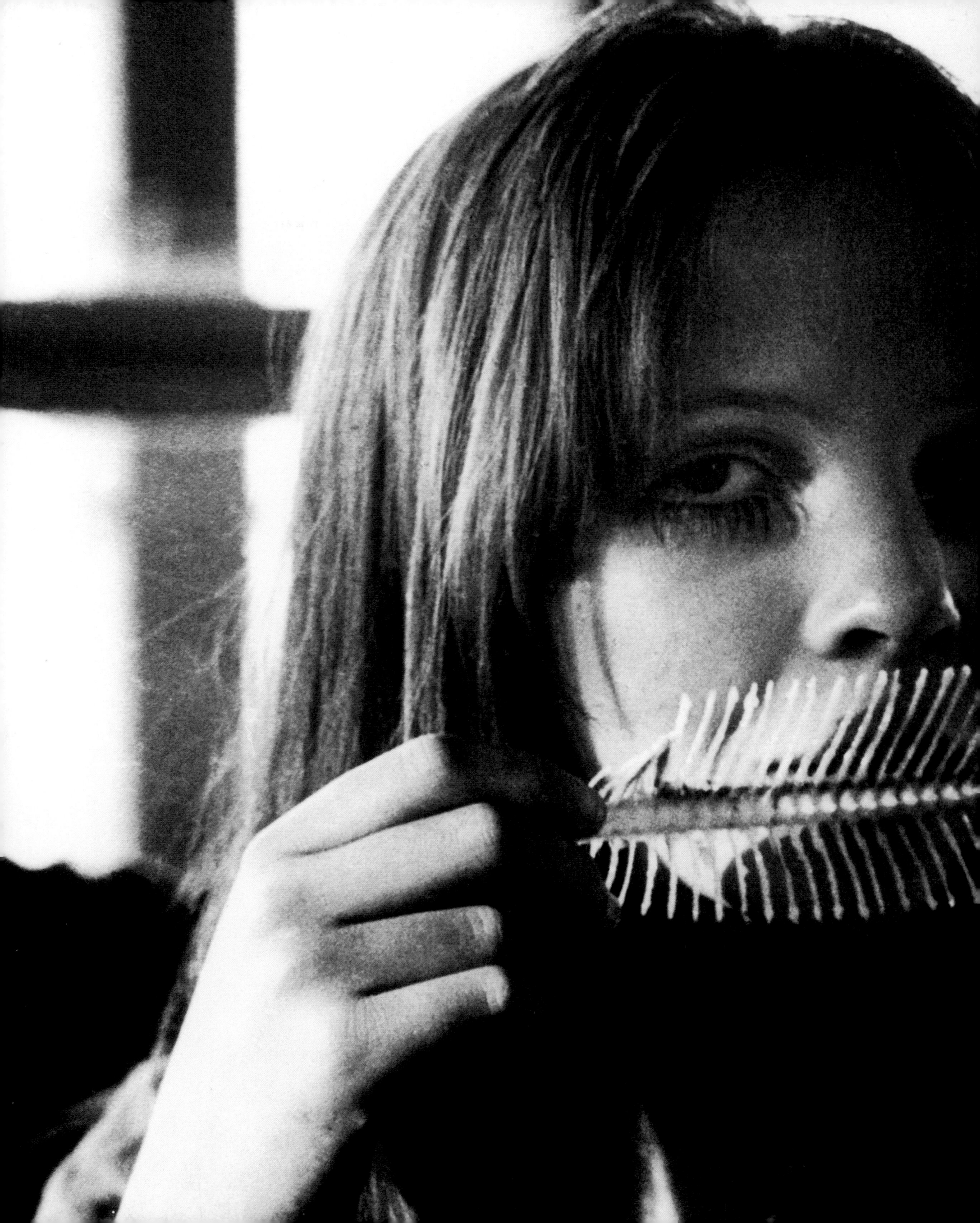

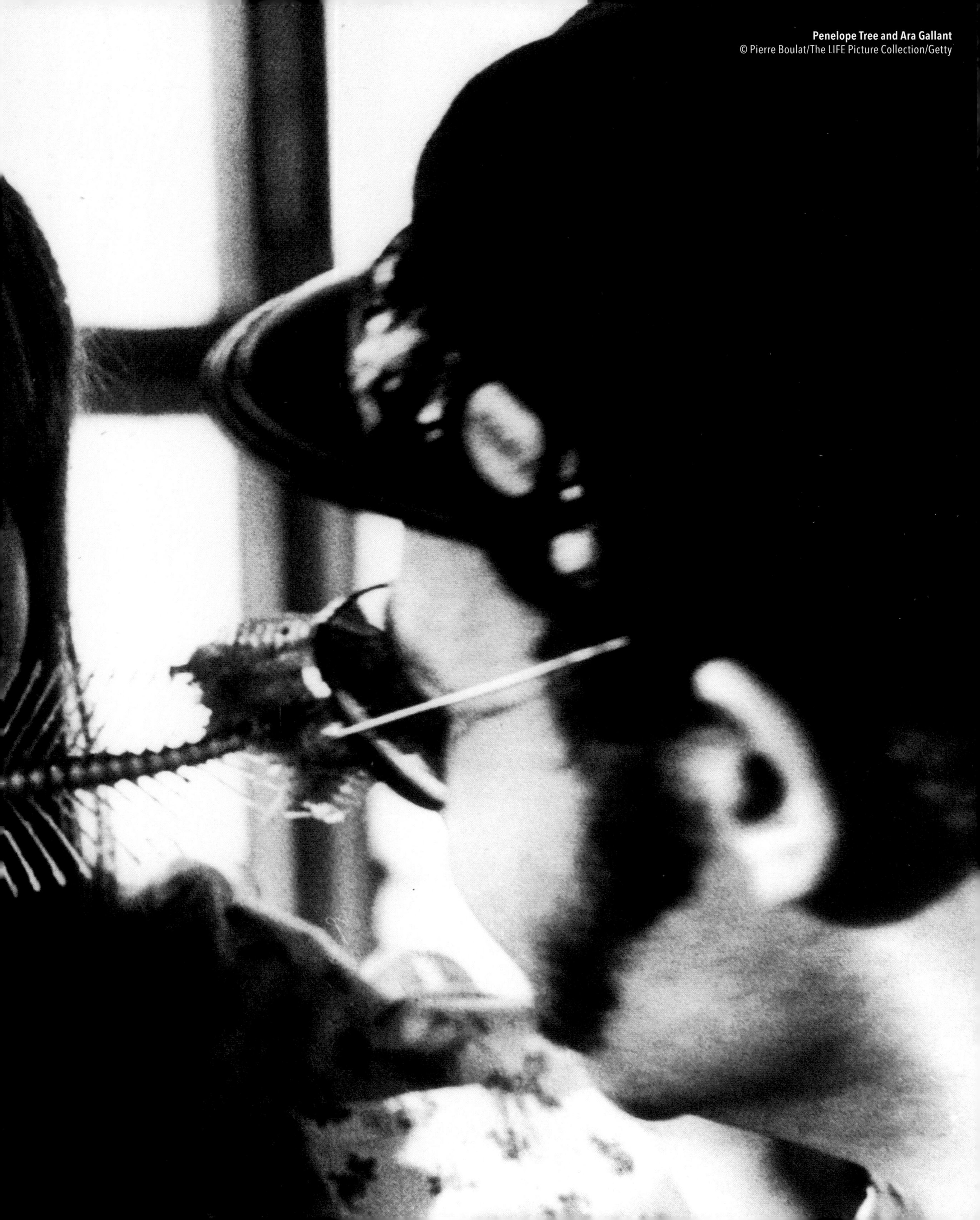

STEVEN MEISEL is an American photographer.

ALEK WEK is a Sudanese–British model and designer who began her career in the 1990s. LUPITA NYONG'O is a Kenyan Academy Award-winning actress.

JERRY HALL is an American model and actress who began her career in the 1970s. LYNN WYATT is an American socialite.

AMANDA LEAR is a French singer, actress, and television personality who began her career as a model in the 1960s. CAROLE SABAS is a French journalist and consultant.

CINDY CRAWFORD is an American model and entrepreneur who began her career in the 1980s. KATIE HOLMES is an American actress and director. © Irving Penn/Condé Nast

MARISA BERENSON is an American actress and model who began her career in the 1960s, under the aegis of Diana Vreeland. DAVID CROLAND is an American illustrator and photographer. © Disney ABC Television Group/Getty

GRACE CODDINGTON is a British fashion editor who began her career as a model in the 1950s. DAVID MONTGOMERY is an American photographer. Terence Donovan © Terence Donovan Archive

LAUREN HUTTON is an American model, actress, and entrepreneur who began her career in the 1960s. JACOB BERNSTEIN is an American journalist.

CARMEN DELL'OREFICE is an American model who began her career in the 1940s. DAVID DOWNTON is a British illustrator. Carmen, hat by Lanvin-Castillo, Pont Alexandre III, Paris, August 1957 © The Richard Avedon Foundation

HEIDI KLUM is a German model, television personality, and entrepreneur who began her career in the 1990s. HARVEY WEINSTEIN is an American Oscar- and Tony-winning producer.

IMAN is a Somali model, actress, and entrepreneur who began her career in the 1970s. EDWARD ENNINFUL is a British fashion editor. © The Francesco Scavullo Foundation / The Francesco Scavullo Trust

APOLLONIA VAN RAVENSTEIN is a Dutch model and actress who began her career in the 1960s. GIAN PAOLO BARBIERI is an Italian photographer.

MARIE HELVIN is a Japanese–American model who began her career in the 1970s. MANOLO BLAHNIK is a Spanish shoe designer.

DONNA MITCHELL is an American model and actress who began her career in the 1960s. CHRISTOPHER NIQUET is a French journalist.

BROOKE SHIELDS is an American model and actress who began her career as a child model in the 1970s. CORNELIA GUEST is an American author, animal rights activist, and designer.

GUINEVERE VAN SEENUS is an American model who began her career in the 1990s. MARC ASCOLI is a French art director.

STELLA TENNANT is a British model who began her career in the 1990s. PLUM SYKES is a British journalist and author.

DONNA JORDAN is an American model who began her career in the 1970s. MARC JACOBS is an American fashion designer.

ERIN O'CONNOR is a British model who began her career in the 1990s.

TIM BLANKS is a New Zealander journalist and author.

CLAUDIA SCHIFFER is a German model who began her career in the 1980s. JUERGEN TELLER is a German photographer.

GENEVIEVE WAITE is a South African actress and singer who began her career as a model in the 1960s. MICHAEL CHOW is a Chinese actor, interior designer, and restaurateur. Genevieve Waite, hair by Ara Gallant, golden butterflies by Robert Originals, New York, August 1970 © The Richard Avedon Foundation

LINDA EVANGELISTA is a Canadian model who began her career in the 1980s. CARLYNE CERF DE DUDZEELE is a French fashion editor and photographer.

INGMARI LAMY is a Swedish model who began her career in the 1960s. KENZO TAKADA is a Japanese fashion designer.

NAOMI SIMS was an American model and entrepreneur who began her career in the 1960s. GOSTA PETERSON is a Swedish photographer.

JANE HOLZER is an American businesswoman and art collector who modeled in the 1960s almost exclusively for Vogue and Diana Vreeland. BOB COLACELLO is an American journalist and author. © Irving Penn/Condé Nast

ANITA PALLENBERG is an Italian actress and artist who began her career as a model in the 1960s. STELLA SCHNABEL is an American actress.

FARIDA KHELFA is a French actress and director who began her career as a model in the 1980s and was a muse to designer Azzedine Alaïa and photographer Jean-Paul Goude. CARLA BRUNI is a French–Italian singer-songwriter and model. Farida, cut-up photograph, Paris, 1983 © Jean-Paul Goude

PAT CLEVELAND is an American model and author who began her career in the 1960s. ZAC POSEN is an American fashion designer. Courtesy Horst Estate/Condé Nast

ANJELICA HUSTON is an American Oscar-winning actress and director who began her career as a model in the 1960s and worked almost exclusively with photographers Richard Avedon, David Bailey, and Bob Richardson. PAMELA GOLBIN is a French curator.

AYUMI TANABE is a Japanese model and designer who began her career in the 1990s. TIFFANY GODOY is an American journalist and consultant.

BEVERLY JOHNSON is an American model, actress, and entrepreneur who began her career in the 1970s. BETHANN HARDISON is an American model, activist, and agent. © Francesco Scavullo/Condé Nast Collection/Getty

PENELOPE TREE is an American activist who began her career as a model in 1960s. PETER EYRE is an American-born British actor. © Condé Nast Ltd-Cecil Beaton/Trunk Archive

ISABELLA ROSSELLINI is an Italian model and actress who began her career in the 1980s. ALAIN ELKANN is an American journalist and author.

PEGGY MOFFITT is an American model who began her career in the 1960s. PAT McGRATH is a British makeup artist and entrepreneur. © William Claxton/Demont Photo Management

CAPUCINE was a French actress who began her career as a model in the 1940s. AMY FINE COLLINS is an American journalist and author.

SUSAN MONCUR is an American model who began her career in the 1960s. SERGE LUTENS is a French photographer and perfumer.

PRINCESS ELIZABETH OF TORO is a Ugandan lawyer who began her career as a model in the 1960s. ADRIENNE KENNEDY is an American Obie-winning playwright. © Irving Penn/Condé Nast

INÈS DE LA FRESSANGE is a French model and designer who began her career in the 1970s and was a muse for the house of Chanel. KARL LAGERFELD is a German fashion designer, photographer, and publisher.

ANH DUONG is a French artist and actress who began her career as a model in the 1980s. CHRISTIAN LACROIX is a French fashion designer, decorator, and costume designer.

LAUREN BACALL was an American actress who began her career as a model in the 1940s. Winner of two Tonys, she was awarded an honorary Academy Award as one of the greatest stars of the Golden Age of Hollywood. JOAN JULIET BUCK is an American journalist and author. © Philippe Halsman/Magnum Photos

VERUSCHKA is a German model and artist who began her career in the 1960s. RICHARD AVEDON was an American photographer. Veruschka, dress by Robert Morton, New York, January 1967 © The Richard Avedon Foundation

CHINA MACHADO is a Chinese–Portuguese model and fashion editor who began her career in the 1950s and was a muse and collaborator of Richard Avedon. LUIS VENEGAS is a Spanish publisher and art director.

RENE RUSSO is an American actress who began her career as a model in the 1970s. SANDY LINTER is an American makeup artist. © The Francesco Scavullo Foundation / The Francesco Scavullo Trust

TERI TOYE is an American model who began her career in the 1980s and was a muse to designer Stephen Sprouse. PAUL CAVACO is an American fashion editor and consultant.

PATTIE BOYD is a British model and photographer who began her career in the 1960s. BARBARA HULANICKI is Polish–British fashion and interior designer.

JEAN SHRIMPTON is an English model who began her career in the 1960s. ANNA SUI is an American fashion designer.

KAREN ELSON is a British model and singer who began her career in the 1990s. CHAN MARSHALL is an American musician who performs under the name Cat Power.

PAULINA PORIZKOVA is a Czech model who began her career in the 1980s. VIRGINIE MOUZAT is a French journalist and author.

NAOMI CAMPBELL is a British model who began her career in the 1980s. ANDRÉ LEON TALLEY is an American journalist and author.

TWIGGY is a British model who began her career in the 1960s. JUSTIN DE VILLENEUVE is a British photographer. © Terry Fincher/Hulton Archive

SUZY PARKER was an American model and actress who began her career in the 1940s. MARTHA STEWART is an American entrepreneur and television personality.

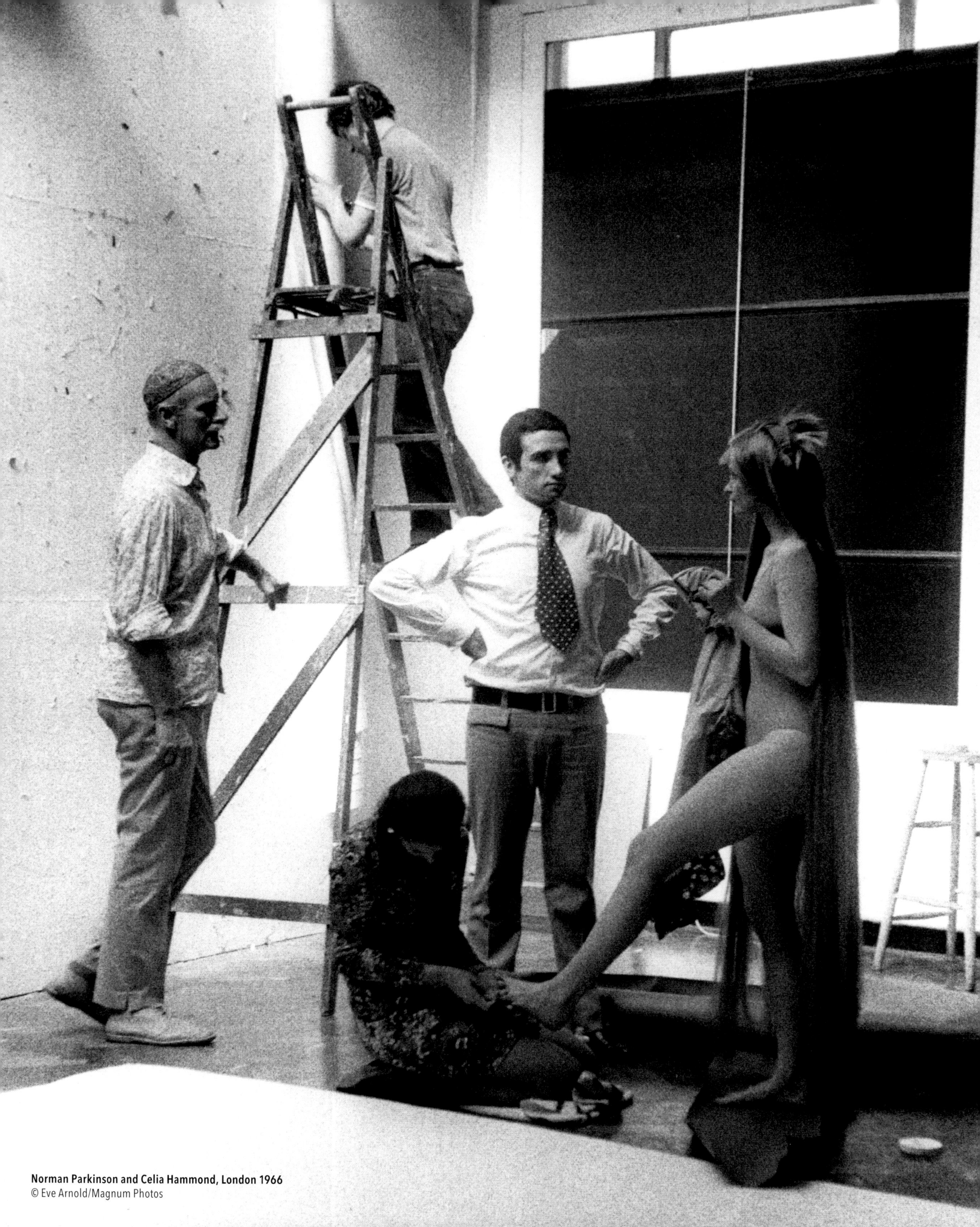

Norman Parkinson and Celia Hammond, London 1966
© Eve Arnold/Magnum Photos

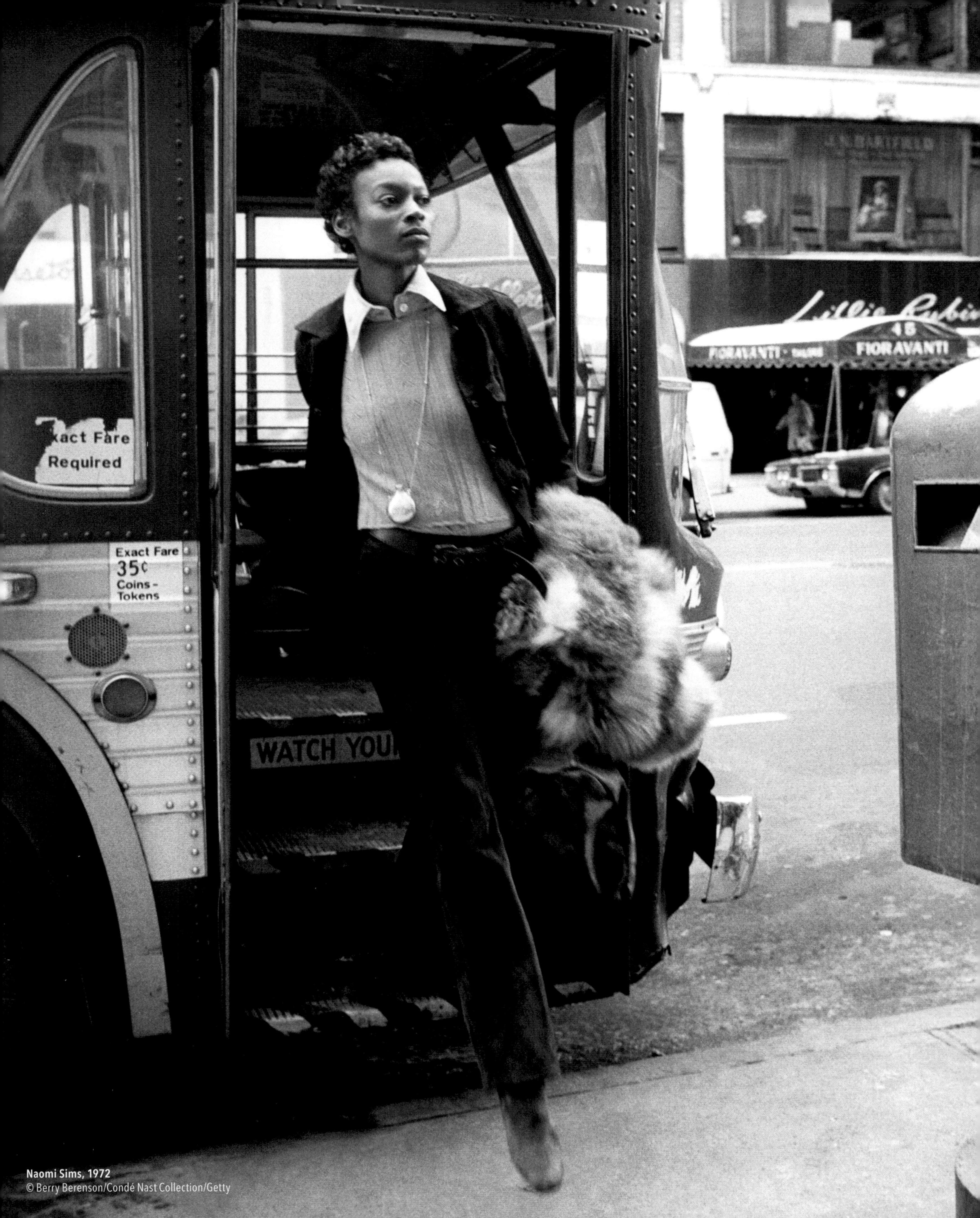

Naomi Sims, 1972

Acknowledgements

All it took was the face of Peggy Moffitt in the deep shadows of Mr. Chow, Beverly Hills, where Karl Lagerfeld was giving a dinner before a Chanel show. Amid the noise, cigarette smoke, and dozens of guests, I was mesmerized: the Sassoon bob, the extreme eye makeup, the graphic stripes of her Gernreich jersey dress. This was 2008, forty-two years after her appearance in Antonioni's *Blow-Up*, but age had hardly changed her. I gathered the courage to ask her for her autograph.

I framed this scrap of memorabilia with a portrait of Peggy taken by her husband, Will Claxton, and hung it in a prime spot above my writing desk in New York. I spent days looking at the twirls that formed her name and strangely mimicked the features of her face. Slowly, a desire grew in me to track down the faces that populated my aesthetic subconscious. A trip to England was spent finding the little inn to which Jean Shrimpton retired; one to California became an obsessive quest for the yoga studio where Ingrid Boulting was teaching. The result was always the same: I gathered a personal memento of a woman who had inspired the fashion gods of her day. The women themselves helped me: Jan Ward put me in touch with Pattie Boyd, Willy van Rooy with Susan Bottomly, and Pat Cleveland with Apollonia van Ravenstein. Each addition to my collection—which now covers the walls of my office—recalled anew the fashions of an earlier time and the people who shaped them.

Most of the great models of past decades still find their way onto the mood boards of fashion designers and advertising photographers, but in the wider world they have become nameless faces. I wanted to bring back a sense of who they were, what made them so special to the people they worked with. This book is my love letter to them.

I would like to thank Steven Meisel for giving me the confidence to turn this personal hall of fame into a book; Joan Juliet Buck for her endless support and *son oeil plus qu'aiguisé et sa fine oreille*; Carole Sabas for her friendship and the introduction to Andrea Albertini of Damiani; and last but not least, Zac Posen.

Christopher Niquet

Christopher Niquet
Models Matter

© Damiani 2016
© Photographs, the Artists
© Text, the Authors

Book Design by
David Schnapper

Published by
Damiani
info@damianieditore.com
www.damianieditore.com

Printed in December 2016 by Grafiche Damiani – Faenza Group SpA, Italy.

ISBN 978-88-6208-519-9